ALSO AVALIABLE FROM PAYROLL
PUBLISHING

Contents

iv

BIANCA

Tell Us Who Did This To You

Inspired by a true story

Payroll Publishing Inc.

First Payroll Publishing paperback printing October 2006

Copyright © 2006 by E. Williams
Published by Payroll Publishing Inc.

ISBN 1-4243-1909-9

Library of Congress Control Number: 2007924282

Cover design by M.S. Graphics

For information regarding special discounts for purchases,
please contact,

Payroll Publishing Inc.
21500 Northwestern HWY suite k-03
Southfield, MI 48075
(248) 996-9805

Printed in the U.S.A

BIANCA

Tell Us Who Did This To You

Inspired by a true story

Payroll Publishing Inc.

__Prologue__

Imagine feeling like a vessel that's used for everybody's pleasure. Imagine always being told "You ain't gonna be nothing but a hoe!" What would this do to your self-esteem as a teenager? Imagine being beat on and then watch your mother get beat throughout your childhood. Do you think you'll grow up to become a violent person yourself? Well Bianca didn't think so, she just had to deal with it.

There were times when Bianca's husband would have her perform oral sex on him and during the act she would be in tears. He really didn't understand what was going on inside of her and many times he told her, "That's okay, you don't have to do this." With a black eye Bianca would look up at him and say she was sorry for being so emotional but her past really bothered her at times. She told him she really wanted to please him and to let her finish doing what she was doing.

But because of all the violence, drugs and her horrific past, Bianca really didn't know what she wanted to do. Violence and sex was all she ever knew. Using her body for the pleasure of those who were close to her was how she was raised. Always having a black eye was the norm for her. Drugs... well the drugs are a whole different story in itself. But one thing is for sure, the shit is about to hit the fan.

Chapter 1

I Remember

My life seemed normal to me at four years old but now I realize it wasn't normal at all. How could it have been normal when I'm now twenty seven years old with 136 cuts on my body that happened in one night? I remember everything that happened to me, and the only reason I'm remembering is because of a situation that happened when I was in Detroit, Michigan. It was during the time of my marriage. I had three kids at the time named Little Keith, L'Tisha and Faith. The situation happened at Little Keith's school, the Pentecostal Church of God Christian Academy.

Evangelist Hart came out to all of the parents' homes of the children who were in grade K. He told us about how they thought someone had been sexually fondling the kindergarteners, and when it came down to my son, it brought up all the memories of what had happened to me.

"Molestation is something big that's happening in our church right now," Evangelist Hart explained to me as I sat in my lounge chair. "God is not pleased with all that stuff and we want to reveal who these people are that's doing such things. So many of us have been molested and raped by people we feel we shouldn't tell on because they may have leadership or something behind their name. Maybe even Pastor or Minister behind their name."

I'll never forget when he got ready to leave he asked me a question.

"Even if somebody has done it to you, you need to reveal it, you need to tell." I felt so hurt knowing somebody could've been molesting my baby. It hurt me so much, to where it brought back memories of my own childhood and made me realize what had happened to me. I didn't reveal anything to Evangelist Hart. Instead I just focused on what he told me. "If it happened to you, you need to reveal it." So I went to bed that night but couldn't sleep because all I could think about was when I was four years old.

I thought about when I was four years old and was sitting on a man's lap while he was rubbing his penis and had my panties pulled down to my thighs. This sick bastard

4

started rubbing his penis up and down the upper part of my butt-crack, and, the crazy thing about it was the fact that I was in love with this man. Not in love the way a woman would love a man, but I was in love with him because I thought he really cared about me the way a father or uncle would. I was raised to care about, love and respect him because he was the Pastor of our church. He was Elder Roosevelt Thomas.

I used to always go over to his house with him and his wife in between church services. They used to call me their "little girl," their "baby." At his house, I was sitting on his lap and he was rubbing his penis in my butt-crack. I turned around and looked to see what he was doing and at the time I had no idea of what a penis was, not even an idea of what a penis looked like. I was totally innocent and just doing what an older person was telling me to do… an older person who was a Pastor and had gray hair. I was taught to do what older people told me to do and to respect what they said. Therefore I had no idea that what was going on was actually wrong.

He gave me a cup and told me to drink my Kool Aid *(it was cherry Kool Aid)*. Then he told me to "Turn around" and when I did I remember something wet splattering on the upper part of my butt. When it happened, I turned around and looked at him as he was shaking while holding his penis

5

in his hand. At the time I didn't know what it was but now I know he was jacking off on me.

When I snapped back to reality I started wheezing and could barley breathe so I got on my nebulizer. I needed some oxygen badly and was sweating from the nightmare I'd just had while wide awake.

The next day I sat around my house and tried to watch television but at that point I was just sitting around remembering. As I sat I could even remember some things like what I ate before I went to the Pastor's house and what he and his wife gave me for dinner. They gave me macaroni and cheese, collard greens, fried chicken and cherry Kool Aid. The Pastor and his wife had children of their own but they were all grown up at the time so I was the only child there.

As I tried to watch television I remembered more things like him having me on his bed and he was trying to put his penis inside my vagina. It was burning and stinging so bad. He tried to make me count to ten but I didn't even know how to count all the way to ten.

"You just count to ten and it'll be over," he kept telling me while on top of me trying to penetrate. Then he switched up and made me get on top of him.

I remember being on top of him and both of us were naked. We were going at it for what seemed to be forever.

He was sweating all over me and then all of a sudden his wife walked in. I'll never forget the expression on her face when she saw the both of us naked. Her mouth just dropped as we both looked at her. I was half asleep by that time. My little body was so drained and wore out. But did she help me? No, she just closed the door and left.

But I didn't feel like I needed any help because when she came in I didn't even reach out to her like, *help me*. I didn't feel like anything was wrong with what was going on. I actually thought it was all normal and okay, especially with her being his wife and coming in and seeing it. With her being a woman I really thought everything was fine.

I had to get ready to go back to church and when I was in the bathroom my vagina was stinging and burning painfully bad. It hurts me to know that I was caring for myself at such a young age. When I look back on it I'm like, *wow, why wasn't I being protected?* I was thinking I was this big happy girl as I wiped myself with some tissue. I even tried to wet the tissue thinking the water would make it stop burning. I was so young but I remember standing on my tippy-toes just to turn the knobs on the sink. That's how short I was. I couldn't even reach the sink. I had to stand on my toes and jump up on the sink to turn on the cold water, not even knowing which one was cold and which one was hot. I turned on the hot water first and got burned when I stuck my hand in it with the tissue. So I had to throw the first tissue away because it had gotten messed up.

I got some more tissue, ran some cold water on it, and when I wiped my vagina there was blood on the tissue from him trying to penetrate me. I didn't think anything of it. This was in-between twelve noon and eight o'clock evening Sunday service. So we went back to church and everything was normal. He gave me a dollar at church then after church I went back home with my mother.

My vagina stung as long as I can remember living in Jacksonville, Florida. Then the stinging stopped once my mother married and we moved to Fort Myers Florida. My mother and everybody who used to keep me knew they couldn't put any soap, detergent, bubble bath or anything in my bath water because it would irritate my vagina. It would burn so bad, and why was it burning? Now that I'm older I'm able to put all the broken pieces back together because it's like a puzzle. I understand who I am now and why I was the way I was growing up.

I sat on my lounge chair and remembered all of this and I started to panic. I paced back and forth around the house for about two hours. My baby was asleep and my son was in school. I felt like I was going to have a nervous breakdown thinking, *how could this happen?* Even though it happened I had never faced it in my adult life.

8

As "church people," we're raised to believe in everything and especially as a child. We believe everything that goes on in church is right. We're made to walk in a straight line, especially when you're dealing with or talking about a Pastor, Elder or someone of the sort. We were raised to respect church people, especially the church leaders. *What he's doing is right.*

"Don't tell nobody," he used to tell me. "We got to keep this between us. This is our little secret." He even teased me by asking, "Oh you gone tell?"

"No I'm not, I promise," I answered him smiling, laughing and not even realizing that I was being scarred for life.

I'm scarred for life and I don't think the scar can ever be healed. Not through counseling, therapy, or even through church. I think God would have to come down himself and give me a new heart for me to be healed. I do think there is a healing process but will I ever be healed? I don't think so. Certain things that happen with me such as sexual activities, I'm not comfortable with because it makes me remember the things he used to do to me.

Another memory of mine is being at his house when I was five years old. I have no idea why I was there but I do know I was actually a little scared that time. Fear had crept in and I was more aware that something could be wrong.

9

He drove me to his house one night after church. When he took me in his house I heard someone yelling and screaming. Another man name Vic Mackeva (a member of the Pentecostal Church of God in Jacksonville, Florida) was walking out of the bedroom, and there was a little boy on the bed. I think what made me so scared was there were two more people there, the little boy on the bed who looked like he was around five or six years old, and Vic. What scared me the most was when the little boy started crying. I looked dead in his face and still to this day I don't know who he was. At age 27 it haunts me to wonder, *who was that little boy?*

"Hey Bianca," Vic asked me.

"Hey," I answered while scared to death because of the little boy who was in the bedroom crying. And he wasn't crying a regular cry. It was a painful cry like he was being hurt.

Elder Thomas took me over to the couch while talking to me.

"The stuff I do with you, I want you to let Vic do it to you," he explained. "Are you my little girl?" he asked me.

"Yes, I'm your little girl," I answered. What's crazy is once he started talking to me I started to feel safe. From his touch I felt a lot more comfortable and that's crazy because he was the one who was scarring me for life by

10

telling me he was going to give me to someone else to let him do to me what he does.

After he gave me to Vic he told him, "Man she's good too, she's good," then they both burst out laughing. Vic wanted me to suck his penis so he took me on the screened in porch where there was just enough light coming in to where nobody could see us. Then he pulled out his penis. I instantly noticed that Vic's penis was much bigger than Elder Thomas' penis and it scared me. But Vic didn't care. He just shoved it in my mouth and made me choke.

I was gagging and choking off his penis because it was way too much to be shoving in my little mouth. So I pulled back and when I did he grabbed a wire hanger then told me if I didn't do it he was going to whup me. He untwisted the hanger then stretched it out the long way and every time I stopped sucking he hit me across my back with it. Therefore I had to keep sucking. I sucked and I sucked until he cums in my mouth.

I started spitting on the floor so much till it was like I was vomiting. I had on a yellow shirt and the cum was all over my shirt. Then he told me to go in the bathroom and clean myself up. When I came back from cleaning myself up Elder Thomas and Vic made me and the little boy have sex with each other… or at least try to have sex with each other. After that Elder Thomas and Vic held me down while Elder

Thomas stuck a Coca Cola bottle in my vagina. Then they bent me over and stuck it in my behind.

One Sunday I was at church and was going to the restroom. Elder Thomas was coming out of the men's room and told me to "Come here," so I went to him. The men's and ladies room both sat side by side. When Elder Thomas told me to "Come here" he made me go into the men's room with him. That's where he straight up stood me on the toilet and made me bend over so he could put his penis in my rectum.

It was hurting too bad so he put his hand over my mouth and told me to, "Shut up! Somebody's going to hear and you're going to get in trouble for being in the boy's bathroom." I knew my grandmother and mother was going to whup me for being in the boy's bathroom so I tried my best to keep quiet. But then I started crying and couldn't stop crying so he stopped. That's when he told me to "Suck it." So I sucked it and sucked it until he came.

Elder Thomas quickly cleaned himself off and made me wash my hands and face off in the men's room. This situation didn't take long because he was rushing and acting real nervous (probably because of someone coming in). Normally when he molested me we were at his house and at his house he wasn't nervous at all.

When I walked out of the men's room an usher was walking out of the church kitchen. Elder Thomas turned around from standing at the sink and started to walk out when the usher saw him.

"I caught her in the men's bathroom, I'm 'bout to tell her mama on her," he told the usher.

"You know better than that!" the usher yelled at me. "Girl I'm 'bout to tell your mama on you! You know you ain't got no business in the boy's bathroom!"

So they told my mother and grandmother and I had to sit in a corner of the kitchen by myself. Then when I got home I got a whuppin' for being in the men's room that he pulled me into.

I remember when I was just little a bit older and Elder Thomas dragged me by my right ankle down to the foot of his bed then put his mouth on my vagina. That was the first time anything like that had happened. It was a really strange feeling to me. He spread my vagina open and his mustache and beard felt like a Brillo Pad on my bare skin. He started moving his head from side to side like he was really getting into it. He became so aggressive with it that for the first time I truly felt the hurt in my heart and knew what was being done to me was most definitely wrong. The room became black to me at that moment and it was like I had left my body. After that day everything went blank and I don't

13

remember any more molesting. That was the day when I repressed everything.

Right around that time my mother was telling me, "Don't let nobody touch your private parts." I guess my mother figured *okay, she's six years old so I guess I can start telling her not to let nobody touch her private parts.* When I was three and four she must have thought I was too young to be introduced to that. But when she started telling me I started feeling the hurt. I was feeling like, *oh my God! My Mama is telling me not to let nobody touch my private parts and I'm letting it happen! But I can't make it stop! He's too big! He's too strong! I can't make him leave me alone!*

Not long after that my mother and I were standing outside of the church one night after an evening service. I was holding on to my mother's hand so tight because she was standing next to Elder and Sister Thomas' car while talking to them. She and Sister Thomas were real cool with each other and I was holding my mother's hand real tight and hiding behind her. I wasn't old enough to know how serious child molestation was but I was old enough to know what he was doing wasn't supposed to be happening.

"Let me get out of here, I don't know what's wrong with this girl," my mother told Sister Thomas. "She's acting like she saw a ghost or something."

Sister Thomas was trying to talk to me while at the same time Elder Thomas was telling me to come on his side of the car. While he was talking to me I was putting my face in the side of my mother's hip.

"You want to go home with me?" he asked me. "Come on and go home with me." I knew what was going to happen if I went home with them so I was scared to death. "Do you want to come over? I thought you said you were my little girl?" He was trying to make me feel guilty but as a child I was already feeling guilty simply because I didn't want to go.

"Girl what's wrong with you? She's squeezing me so tight," my mother told Sister Thomas. But fortunately I didn't go with them.

For a long time after that I thought every man I saw in a white wife beater T-shirt was going to get ready to do something sexual to me. That's because those were the types of shirts he wore under his church suits. That was the way he normally presented himself to me, in a wife beater T-shirt.

Chapter 2

I Would've Been Better Off

The molestation ended when we moved. My mother married a man in Fort Myers, Florida and we moved in with him. Even the stinging I kept feeling in my vagina stopped. But at that time in my life I really wasn't aware of, *hey, I've been molested*. At that time I had repressed it. But I used to always wonder, *why now all of a sudden I can put bubbles in my water?*

I was seven when my mother got married so all of the molestation took place between the age of three and six. And I think if I would've stayed in that city I would've stayed a victim because the molesters go to our church. We have these big meetings and conventions and when we moved every time he would look at me in church I would always be scared of him. I mean really scared of him, and I never gave it any thought as to why I was scared of him because I had repressed it. When he would "Praise the Lord" with me I would shake, even when I made it to my teenage years around sixteen or seventeen.

I would shake and tremble when I would see him in the back area of the Convention Center where the restrooms were. When I spotted him, I would try to wait for him to leave or I would go get one of my cousins to walk in there with me. And at every church convention he said something to me, every single service. And I believe the reason he was doing that was because he was trying to see if I remembered, or to make sure that we were cool and I wouldn't tell.

Years later when I was eighteen, we were at a church convention and Elder Thomas walked up to me while we were in the kitchen. His wife was within a few footsteps away from us and she was buying something from the scholarship foundation table. That's when he walked up to me and shook my hand.

"Praise the Lord. Girl I ain't seen you in a long time. Hey, why don't you come back to Jacksonville with me to have sex because I haven't had sex in a long time?" I was eighteen years old at the time and that scared me. I hadn't even thought anything about the fact that he had molested me. At the time I just wondered why would he say something to me like that?

Why would he just come at me like that? He's the Pastor and an Elder. He has a position but that didn't stop him. And when he shook my hand and praised the Lord with me I tried to pull away, but then he squeezed my hand so tight that he left a bruise on it and his hand print was on my hand.

I was dating a guy name Garry Tucker and when I got in his car I told him all about it. I also told my mother and she told my aunt who told Sister Ross (the Bishop's wife). After telling I had to go see Sister Ross and when I told her what happened she said she was going to make sure Bishop Ross knows about it. But nothing was ever done about it. The situation was treated like, *what the fuck ever*.

A bunch of young men who are my age and from the city of Jacksonville *(about ten of them)* all grew up struggling with their sexuality, then turned out to be gay. One day I was talking to a friend of mine, let's just call him Carter. Carter's brother is one of the gay guys and we were all on the three-way when I broke down crying about everything. I never talked to Carter on that level but when I told him my story he was like, "Man, ain't that a bitch! You wonder why all these guys turned out to be gay?" And believe it or not, Elder Thomas' name came up.

When Carter's brother started to tell us why these guys were gay it went like this:

"Well who molested him?"

"Well that person did it to him." It was another young guy who molested him.

"Well who did it to him?"

"This person did it to him."

"Who did it to that person?"

"Elder Thomas did it to him." He was the root of it all, and it's crazy because that motherfucker is still there! Over twenty years later he's still there! At the same church!

Now that I'm older I know from experience that I was having orgasms when Elder Thomas was molesting me. Can you imagine what that's like to experience an orgasm at three, four and five years old? Some people say, "No, that don't exist," but that's bullshit. I was having orgasms when I was being molested and I always knew that feeling that felt so good to me. As a little girl sometimes I would sit on the toilet and try to get that feeling back. It's real sickening but you have to understand I had been fondled with. I thought once I got married and started having sex with my husband the feeling would change to something greater. Then after we had sex I was like, *wow, there's nothing new, it's that same old feeling.* There was nothing surprising because I had been having that same feeling since I was a little kid.

Later on in my life there was a time I was performing oral sex on my husband and I just bust out crying. It was like the molestation was happening to me all over again. That's why I say molestation will scar you for life. You think there's a healing point, you believe there's a healing point, but when you're almost healed there's always something that brings it back up again: especially when you go to the same church where the molester is. Every time someone mentions the Pentecostal Church of God all I think about is him.

Even when I don't go to church my family members will come home from church and talk about him. It's a lot of things I don't get because I told my mother this happened to me and she's still cool with him and his wife right now to this day. There's no way one of my kids can tell me they were molested and I'll still be cool with their molester. My mother is in some photos with them at the Bishop's Appreciation and she still talks to them on the phone! I almost hated my mother for that shit but she can't help it. She's fucked up in the head her damn self and I don't think nobody knows this except for me and God.

Sometimes I think I would've been better off left in Jackson with the molester because my life only got harder when my mother got married. I was always in a domestic violent and child abusive situation in my home. My own mother wasn't doing nothing about it so growing up I began to think there was nothing to be done about it. I went from being molested to being abused, me and my little brother.

When I was seven my mother married a man from the Pentecostal Church of God name Minister Fred Cooley. We then moved to Fort Myers, Florida. There was another man in the picture name Bonnie Barker from Winter Haven, Florida. To me the marriage didn't seem to be too sacred or serious because my mother allowed me to make the choice of which man she was to marry.

"Which one should I marry, Bonnie or Minister Cooley?" she asked me. I chose Minister Cooley because I didn't want to live in Winter Haven. It was a place nobody wanted to be. We hated Winter Haven growing up as kids. We stayed at the church motel during church conventions and the motel was some real bullshit. We hated that shit.

I remember the first time Minister Cooley beat me. I was only eight years old. It was as if he already had it out for me anyway. I sensed that he wanted to beat me for a long time. You ever felt like somebody just wanted to do something to you, like you know this person wanted to fight you? That's how big of a grudge he had against me.

We were in a church convention called the Bishop's Council. During that convention we were staying at the

Holiday Inn Hotel. My mother left me and a few of my cousins in the room so Minister Cooley could watch us. He was telling us to stop making noise, and to stop playing, and for me to pick up something from under the table. We were doing what he said and while doing it we were still laughing but not as loud. Then he got a belt that he worked in which had cement and plaster matted on it, and without a warning he just started beating me.

After the beating I had bruises all over my entire body. I thought he was way out of line for beating me the way that he did while my mother wasn't there. Plus, he wasn't my real father. He was only my step-father. That was my first beating and as time went on, me, my little brother and my mother all got beatings.

At that time my little brother was only four years old and he wasn't Minister Cooley's son either. But one day we were at the laundry mat and Minister Cooley and my mother got into a fight. He picked her up and tried to put her in the car causing her to bust her ear because he tried to throw her in while she was struggling. When he got her in he walked to the driver's side of the car then she got out of the car and started walking. He started driving all wild and crazy to catch up with her so she broke out running. Minister Cooley pulled alongside of her and hit her with the car and all of this was traumatizing to us two young kids in the back seat.

My little brother Deon had his hands on his ears screaming with his face in my lap. I was rubbing his back and telling him everything was going to okay. From that day on it was like I became his protector from everybody in the family because they were just so weak. They were so weak till it fucked them up really bad.

Not long after that my mother and Minister Cooley were in their bedroom arguing and fighting. I came out of my room and saw a bloody knife on the table and from all of the loud arguing I became scared. But even as a child I had to think, and think quickly.

I went into my room to plan out something to do. Because I saw the bloody knife on the table I wondered, *what can I do to make this stop?* So I started screaming really loud until the both of them ran into my room.

"What's wrong?" they asked.

"Grandma, its Grandma!" I screamed.

"What?"

"Grandma, I think she's dead!"

"What are you talking about?"

"I just had a dream and Grandma is dead!"

I was making it up just to get the two of them to stop fighting, and it worked. They got on the phone and called my Grandma for me then went back into the room like two civilized people. Minister Cooley grabbed the knife off the table and took it into the kitchen on the sly like I didn't see it. But I had already seen it.

As I was growing up, me and Minister Cooley didn't get along at all. How could I get along with a man who had the title of a Minister and I constantly saw him fighting and beating on my mother?

There was another situation where he was beating her so bad that it sounded just like it does when a person gets punched on TV. I was hearing the punches come out of their bedroom. Their bedroom door had a square whole in the center with a curtain on it. I pulled the curtain back and he had my mother by her hair punching the shit out of her and as he was punching her blood was flying out of her mouth.

I was scared to death when I saw what was going on so I ran out the front door then started running down the street. As I was running Minister Cooley ran out the house yelling, "Bianca! Where are you going?" but I kept running and didn't look back.

I ran to some church people's house not too far from our house and told them, "If they come looking for me tell them I'm not here!" Then I hid in their closet and stayed there. Eventually my parents came over and I had to leave. As they drove me back home they told me they were sorry. Even when we arrived home, we sat on the couch and he said he was sorry and it wouldn't happen again. I just sat there and cried because I had just seen my mother get her faced bashed in. He told me it wouldn't happen again but that was some bullshit because it continued to happen, over and over again, then we'll go to church and he'll preach about the Lord this and Lord that.

How can he get up and talk about the Lord when he can't even control his own self? He was the most violent person that I had ever seen at that point. And I'm not talking about the little violence they show on TV with these women getting slapped and pushed around. That's not domestic violence to me. What I'm talking about is a man knocking my mother's teeth out with his fist to the point where she had to get dentures at a young age.

I'll never forget one day I walked into the bathroom and my mother was standing at the sink holding her lip up and crying. When I looked at her it scared the hell out of me because her face was all black and blue. Her teeth were gone and blood was all over the sink and floor.

"Mom, are you okay?" I asked when I walked in.

"Get out!" she yelled then slammed my finger in the door. "Get out of here! Get out! Don't come back in here no more, get out!"

I was only trying to help her but situations like that have me traumatized still to this day. Every time I think about it it's like, *what the hell? There's not that much forgiveness in the world! But for some reason she's still with that motherfucker!* I know the truth about everything that has happened, she knows the truth and he knows the truth. Maybe that's the reason why Minister Cooley can't look me in my face to this day.

Deon was seeing all of this traumatizing shit also and would wet the bed because of it. Every time he would wet the bed Minister Cooley would tell him he was going to wake him up with a belt and beat him.

Minister Cooley got up for work at five a.m. then he would go into my little brother's room to check on him. Naturally my brother wet the bed because he would go to sleep in fear because they were arguing, fighting, throwing stuff, busting glass, outside breaking windshields, and all while he's in his room trying to go to sleep by himself. So as early as five in the morning Minister Cooley just started beating him. He didn't even wake him up first. My little brother got woken up with the belt, and then he had to take a bath and go back to bed.

When Minister Cooley would go to work I would let my little brother come into my room and I'd put peroxide on his cuts. He was being beat so bad to where his skin was ripped open and he was bleeding all over the place. My mother and brother were afraid of Minister Cooley, but at that time I wasn't and he knew it. He knew I wasn't afraid of him so it was like I became his main target.

I began to feel like I had to protect my little brother because he was so young and helpless, a victim. All throughout middle school and some of high school I would stay awake for as long as I could, playing my keyboard and writing songs until it was time for me to go to school. Sometimes I would stay awake for two and three days because I was trying to protect my little brother. If I did sleep it was only for thirty minutes to an hour then I would get up and put my little brother on the toilet so he wouldn't wet the bed.

I used to tell my cousins and some other family members about some of the things that went on in our house but nobody ever believed me. That's until a couple of my cousins stayed over one weekend and my parents started fighting while we were sitting in the living-room. Minister Cooley was dragging my mother from the kitchen through the dining-room to the living-room, beating her silly.

Even after that, Minister Cooley would complain to my grandmother about me.

"Bianca is just disrespectful," he complained. "She's just rude. She don't wanna listen to me because I'm not her real daddy. She don't have no respect for me."

They would sit right at the dinner table and talk about me in front of the whole family. So after that I had to hear it from everybody in the family. When we went to church my uncles would look at me mean. One of my self-righteous uncles pulled me aside and said, "You need to listen to what your step-daddy say! Y'all ain't even his kids! At least you could respect a man in his house!"

They didn't know shit! All of them were on the outside looking in. Let somebody bash their mother's head in and see if they're going to respect that motherfucker. That's why people shouldn't judge other people's situations. If you ain't in it then shut the fuck up!

Eventually the whole family found out that Minister Cooley was beating my mother. One day my grandmother and my aunt were over when they broke out fighting again. They were in their bedroom where he was beating her and she started screaming out to her mother and sister, "Mama! Mama! Mama! Donna! Donna!" she screamed at them for help.

My aunt was getting up to go into the room and help her when my grandmother stopped her.

"You can't help her because she don't want to help herself," my grandmother told my aunt. "She act like she so in love with this man but she in love with his money."

And that was that. They didn't do anything about it. They felt like she was staying with a man who was dogging her, beating her like crazy, mistreating and beating her kids, and she was with him because he made good money. And maybe they were right.

I should hate my mother for letting us grow up in that bullshit home. It was enough for me to walk away and hate her for the rest of my life. But I don't because she's my mother, so that's how we lived and it was some real bull shit.

Chapter 3

Cooley Is Out To Get Me

There was a time when Sister Greer came to Fort Myers, Florida to run a meeting. Sister Greer was the national supervisor of the Women's Department for the Pentecostal Church of God. On the Saturday of the meeting we were going to go out and sell Krispy Cream Donuts for the scholarship foundation. That morning Minister Cooley came into my room to wake me up.

I was lying there in a slip and my breast was out. He woke me up by feeling on my breast. Of course he denied it but he did it. I'm a light sleeper and anything wakes me up, especially somebody touching me. He reached out and felt on my breast...but I was made out to be liar by my mother and him. When I opened my eyes and saw him touching my breast he jumped back and tried to act like he was touching my shoulder. "Bianca, Bianca, wake up," he tried to play it off.

After I got up and dressed myself, I went to the church. Sister Greer noticed that I was mad as hell so I told her what happened. She then told the Pastor who was Elder Conner. The pastor told Bishop Ross who's the Bishop of District #4 *(The Pentecostal Church of God in Florida and California)*. Bishop Ross called me, my mother and Minister Cooley into his office, and this was the day my mother put something between us that can never be moved.

"Is this so, did this happen?" Bishop Ross asked me.

"Yes Sir Bishop Ross," I answered.

At that time I had so much respect for the "Man of God" that I wasn't about to lie to him. I was a teenager then and at the time everybody was saying, "You don't lie to Bishop, he knows when you're lying." So I told him the truth.

"Bianca, I did this to you? You're lying!" Elder Cooley said.

"Okay, but you did it though."

"I don't think she'll keep saying you did if you didn't," Bishop Ross commented. "Why would she keep saying you did it?"

I was not about to let it go. I was not about to leave out of there saying he didn't do it because he was trying to overpower me as an adult. An adult trying to outtalk a kid, that's easy. But fuck that, motherfucker you did it! But he was so persistent on saying he didn't do it and this is what made me have a problem with my mother because she straight up jumped to his defense.

Me and him were going back and forth,

"No I didn't!"

"Yes you did!"

"No I didn't!"

"Yes you did! I ain't changing 'cause it's the truth!" The truth is just the truth and you can't change the truth. I didn't want it to be true, but it was true! You think I wanted something like that? Hell naw! Then I had to go back home and live with his domestic violent ass! Do you know how scared I was of going home that day?

"I know I'm gonna get a whuppin'," I told Bishop Ross.

"For what?" he asked me.

"For telling the truth."

"Don't whup her, Bishop Ross told him. "Ain't nobody gonna whup you." *That's what you think*, I sat there and thought to myself. "Well Sister Cooley, what do you think about this?"

"I think she's lying!"

When she said that I thought to myself, *motherfucker, this is your chance to tell, not only what he did to me but what he's done to you!* She was twofaced because she would get in the car with me and tell me she was leaving him.

"One day he's gonna come home and we'll be gone!" I was happy because she was talking about leaving that motherfucker. "Old black bastard!" that was her favorite thing to call him. "You black bastard!"

We were talking about how we were going to get away, now you get in the office and switch on me! If that would've been today I would've hit her. God forbid, I would've tried to knock the shit out of my own Mama. She chose a man over her daughter. She chose what he had to say over what I was telling her which was the truth!

"Why do you think she's lying?" Bishop Ross asked my mother.

"Because she can't stand him. She don't like him because he's not her real daddy."

Right at that moment I closed up and wouldn't talk or tell. I went into a shell because I felt betrayed by my own fucking Mama. Bishop Ross kept talking to me but I wouldn't respond.

"Bianca if you don't talk to me I can't help you."

Talk to you for what? I looked at it as if my own mother didn't have my back then who was going to protect me? If she didn't believe me then why would he? Who the fuck was there for me to depend own? Just thinking back on it I hate my mother for that. She could've saved me from so much other stuff that went on after that.

When we got back home everything seemed like it was so bad. I was going to school every day straight up not even wanting to live and praying something bad happened to me. I felt worthless, like what's the purpose of me being here? I had some crazy love for God but at times I felt like even he had betrayed me. I felt like he had forsaken me. *How do you allow this Lord? I guess the Lord won't put nothing on me that I can't bear,* I thought to myself.

After that the verbal and physical abuse towards me became worse. The man had it out for me. Some of the names he called me were a failure and a whore. He'd call me a whore straight up in front of everybody in the house. "She ain't gonna be nothing but a hoe!" Why did I have to be a hoe? I guess because I wouldn't give him none of my pussy?

My grandmother once told me, "The only reason he didn't take it no further is because he knew you would tell.

It's because of your mouth. You always had a big mouth." If I hadn't opened my big mouth and said something that same morning it happened, only God knows what he would've tried to do to me. If I would've acted scared when I looked into his eyes, he probably would've started raping me. There were many nights when I had to sleep fully dressed in that uncomfortable house.

I used to run away from home to my boyfriend Garry Tucker's house. I used to tell him about the different stuff I was going through but that was unnecessary because he could always see the bruises on my body. One day we were at church and he saw a bruise on my leg and asked, "Did Minister Cooley do that?" I had bruises all over me but he could only see the one on my leg. When I showed him my arm he said, "Minister Cooley needs his ass kicked!"

Then people started seeing for themselves how the man hated me. We were at choir rehearsal one day and they claimed I was the best singer in the church. I normally sang soprano but that day I was asked by the choir director to sing alto. So I did what I was asked to do. Minister Cooley was in the back of the church with the Brothers watching everything.

"I can't hear y'all!" the choir director shouted. "I can't hear y'all! Sing louder! Sing louder!"

Next thing I know Minister Cooley walked up and pushed me in my back, straight up in the church in front of everybody.

"You ain't singing!" he shouted.

"I am singing! She told me to sing alto!" Then he pushed me to the floor so hard that I sprung my arm and busted my fucking mouth. Right in the fucking church abuse was happening. All those fucking church people were sitting right there and not a damn thing was done about it. That was some real bullshit.

After throwing me to the floor he took me outside. My nose was bleeding, the top of my lip was busted, my fucking arm was sprung and I had a knot on my head. He told me he was sorry and a bunch of other bullshit, then he started talking about the Lord.

"I'm not always right, but the Lord wants to use you. You got a beautiful voice and can sing better than anybody in that church. You can out sing all those people in there and I know you can sing louder than that. But I didn't hear her tell you to sing alto." Then he made me go right back to my same spot and sing in front of everybody while another motherfucker brought me some ice for my lip.

I was embarrassed and humiliated and from that day on our personal business was just out there. Everybody knew that our house was a dysfunctional home. "Oh, Minister

Cooley is beating Sister Cooley," was what they said amongst themselves. Then they started having sympathy for me but I was still living in a house with a man who hated me.

He was out to get me. He couldn't stand my popularity. He couldn't stand that I was so outgoing. He couldn't stand that every man in the church wanted to fuck me. Every boy wanted to fuck me. Every nigga we passed in the street wanted me, man I was beautiful! But at the time my self-esteem was low. I was beautiful and didn't know it.

♫ ♫ ♫ ♫ ♫

My mother and Minister Cooley had two more children when I was a teenager. Minister Cooley never abused his real kids because they were his pride and joy.

I'll never forget the day when he took my baby brother Derrick *(his son)* and held him in front of me and Deon after cussing and fighting with our mother and had whupped us. "You see this?" he shouted. "This is my son! This is my blood! I'll never love y'all the way I love my own!"

Ain't that some shit to say to some kids? You should never say some shit like that to some kids. At the time he had been promoted to Pastor of the church in Plant City, Florida, and he told us some shit like that. No longer Minister Cooley but now he was Elder Cooley and called himself a "Man of God" while making a division in his home.

One day I couldn't take it anymore and ran away from home, again. I went to Garry's house and not long after my parents came looking for me with the police. Garry's parents (*Deacon and Sister Tucker*) my parents, plus Garry and I were standing on the porch while the police were talking to me.

"You know what we do to runaways?" the police asked me.

"No Sir, I don't know."

"We take them to a children's home. You'll have to live in a foster home. But this is your choice. You get to go home to your beautiful family and your bed, or get in the car with us then go downtown and get put in a home. We'll book you in and sign you over to the State."

I had a choice to make. Either go back home with Elder Cooley and my mother or go with the police. Which one do you think I chose? It was scary seeing the police and the red and blue lights flashing from the police car, but I still jumped in the back of the police car.

"Something must be really wrong with this home if this child doesn't want to go back," the officer commented. Even they could see.

No child is going to jump in the back of the police car instead of jumping in the back of her parent's car! *Fuck that, take me to jail,* was what I was thinking.

"She think she's grown take her to jail!" my mother yelled. "Scare her up! Let her see what it's like! She wanna be grown, she wanna jump in the back of the police car and go with y'all!" My mother and Elder Cooley were telling the officers to rough me up and take me through a lot of bullshit.

"We're going to make it to where she wants to go home," one officer said. "Come on and get in! Let me show you what happens to young people like you."

"What's going on in your home that you don't want to go back?" the other officer asked as if he didn't understand.

I didn't answer the officer's question and in fact, I should've been scared to death. But I felt good and safe in the back of that police car like a criminal. At that age I had a lot of respect for the police and was blind to the reality of corrupted cops. All I knew was when I saw cops they were coming out to my school talking about "Officer friendly. We're there for you when you're in trouble." Well take me wherever y'all have to take me but don't take me back to that house.

I exhaled for the first time in a long time in the back of that police car. I was happy and tears of joy were rolling down my face.

They took me to the so-called rough side of Fort Myers, Florida, which was named Anderson but was renamed Martin Luther King Blvd. We went to some abandoned homes where people were smoking rocks. As they were walking and talking to me I was trying to only tell them certain things I wanted them to know. I knew if I told them everything they were going to take my mother's kids away from her.

"You don't want to end up like this. You don't want this type of life for yourself do you?" the officers asked.

"Naw, I don't want that," I answered as they pointed out some prostitutes.

"These women get beat up out here. You don't want to experience that."

"Well, I've already experienced getting beat up."

"Who beat you up?" I stopped talking at that point. "We can't help you if you don't talk to us." The officer zipped up my jacket then squatted on his knees. "Honey, we're here to help you. If something's going on in your home...I know it's something going on in your home for you to choose to come with us instead of going with your mother. Was she your real mother?"

"Yes, she's my real mother."

"Is that your real father?"

"No, he's my step-father."

"Tell me, I know something is wrong."

I didn't tell him anything so they took me to a girl's home. In the girl's home I was very anti social and kept my distance from the other girls. There was a piano there so I sat at it and started playing. I loved the music and played by ear without ever being taught. Then before I knew it, all eyes were on me.

"Oh, she plays the piano," one of the women who worked there blurted out. "Honey you have such a big future ahead of yourself. You're going to be successful one day"

Everybody who met me believed that I was going to be successful in my music career. "You're so talented. You're so gifted." But playing the piano helped me to open up and be more social to the people there. I explained to them how I learned to play and what church I went to. But eventually the woman talked me into going back home.

"I bet your little brother misses you," she told me and "brother" was the key word.

I went back for Deon and he probably never knew it. When she mentioned him my heart started beating so fast while I thought, *damn I left him!* Then I started thinking about all the horrible things Elder Cooley was doing to him, that evil creature. So I went back feeling like I couldn't be broken.

♫ ♫ ♫ ♫ ♫

By the ninth grade I was attending the school of the arts and was making good grades. I used to sign people's year books along with a close friend of mine *(even though we were freshmen)* because they just knew we were going to be famous. The seniors told me if I wasn't going to be a singer then I was going to have my own talk show. Everybody just knew I was going to be something. But now look at me. I'm a nobody trying to tell everybody about some bullshit that I've been through.

One day I was doing my homework and listening to the air-conditioner rattle our old window when all of a sudden I heard a loud "Boom!" The first thing I thought was my mother's mirror fell off the dresser because it wasn't attached all the way. I didn't hear any yelling or fussing so that's what I thought. I ran into her bedroom and before I could say 'are you alright,' Elder Cooley had my mother down on the floor punching her. Soon as he saw me open the door he picked up his tennis shoe, threw it in my face as hard as he could, and then told me to "Get the fuck out!"

42

He had told me before if they were ever fighting I better not ever come in and try to help my mother. I was younger when he told me that. It was right after they had finished fighting and I had ran in the room screaming, "Stop! Stop! Leave my Mama alone!" We all sat down to talk about what they were acting stupid over when he told me that bullshit right in front of her.

"We're grown and if you ever see us fighting you just stay out of it."

"Yeah Bianca, you just stay out of it," she said with him.

Elder Cooley hit me in my face with his shoe so hard that the next morning I went to school with his shoe print on face. By that time I had seriously had enough. When I arrived at school I wrote my vocal assemble teacher a letter saying how my mom and step-father were fighting all night and I didn't get any sleep. So could she please excuse me because I wanted to lie down and get some rest because I was tired and sleepy?

Before I knew it I was called down to the office and the Social Service had gotten involved. Social Services called my mother and told her they were coming to check her home to make sure her kids weren't being abused. I was scared as hell and thought I was really going to get in trouble because my mother was going to get her kids taken away.

43

When I got home my mother and Elder Cooley were fussing and fighting again because of the letter I gave to my teacher. I stayed in my room that whole day then went back to school that next morning. That afternoon I got an emergency phone call on the classroom phone from my mother.

"Hello," I answered after my teacher gave me the phone.

"Bianca, I hope you're happy!" my mother yelled. "I hope you realize what kind of damage you did! I knew this was what you wanted all along! Thanks to you these people are coming to take my kids! They taking you, they taking all my kids away from me!"

"But Mama, but it did happen."

"But it's all because of what you wrote in that letter and what you told them!"

"But Mama it really happened. It happened."

Throughout my life they had me believing and feeling like I was the sick person, like I was the one with the problem, and I was the crazy one when they were the sick individuals. Do you know how crazy that is when you're living with some dysfunctional people and they're trying to make you be the one who's crazy?

But my mother was on the phone crying and straight up flipping out.

"I hope you happy! If I ain't gonna have my kids then it ain't no reason for me to live! I'm just gonna go and kill myself! I'm committing suicide!"

"No Mama!" I screamed alerting all the other kids in the classroom.

"I want you to know I'm going to just kill myself! I'm just gonna go and jump off a bridge! I'm going to kill myself! I hope you happy! You won't have to worry about me, you won't have to worry about him! You'll have a new mama and a new daddy!"

After she told me she was going to kill herself, I ran and grabbed my book-bag then told my friend David to drive me home. By that time the Dean and all of the other school officials were looking for me. They spotted me running down the hall and yelled out for me but I kept running. I was cut off by the assistant principle before I ran out of the door.

"Bianca calm down!"

"No I gotta go home! My Mama is finna kill herself! I gotta go home!"

It was the worse feeling in the world to be sitting in my classroom and get a call from my mother saying she was about to kill herself. I felt like if I didn't get there in enough time she was going to be dead. All I was thinking was when I got home she was going to be dead. But when I made it home she was okay. The situation scarred me for life and every time I think about it, it does something to my insides.

A woman from the church came over to stay with my mother for a while and I ended up going to her house. While I was there my mother called me and said the only way they weren't going to take her kids was if I go back to school and tell them I lied.

"Well, I know it's true," my mother told me. "You know it's true, but what goes on in this house stays in this house."

That was some bullshit! Some of the things that went on in our house didn't need to stay in our house. Shit needs to be revealed or you'll have people like me who grow up and be scarred for life.

So I had to go back to school and say I lied. I had to ruin my reputation with the school officials. We had to sit in a meeting with some social workers and I had to make up a big lie so my mother could keep her kids. I had to sit there and get chewed out by this one social worker.

"Bianca, it's not good for you to make up things like this! You could've had your mother in a whole lot of trouble because the State was ready to come in and take all of you away!"

I was feeling like shit because I thought I was ruining my reputation at the school. The people there knew me and when we walked out of the meeting the head principle tapped me on my shoulder and said, "Bianca it's going to be alright. I know you weren't lying. If you ever need somewhere to go here's my number." My teacher just looked at me as if she believed me and that made me feel so good that tears filled my eyes. "If there's one thing we know you're not, we know you're not a liar."

To live in that domestic violent and abusive home was hell enough, and for my mother to make me out to be a liar when the shit was really happening was even worse. They stood before the "people of God" and the "Man of God" and said that it didn't happen, and for somebody to believe me was the only thing I wanted in the first place.

Right after that, my teacher came over to our house and had a talk with me and my mother.

"Bianca is such a good student and such a good girl. We don't have any problems out of her and everybody loves her. Bianca is popular and so smart. She's so talented and gifted. Do you know how good your daughter can sing? Bianca is going to be famous one day. She's going to be on Oprah."

There were a bunch of positive things she told my mother and it was like *so what*. What my teacher said about me didn't mean shit because the house was too dysfunctional for anybody to notice that, *hey, Bianca is talented, or Bianca is gifted.*

♫ ♫ ♫ ♫ ♫

There was another situation that happened when I was between fourteen and fifteen years old. I had gotten pregnant by Garry and when my mother and Elder Cooley found out, I was already three months into the pregnancy. They had Garry come over and we all had a meeting in the living-room. They asked us what were we going to do about the situation and was he going to be there for the baby?

"Bianca, what are you going to do?" Elder Cooley asked me.

"I'm going to take care of it."

I didn't know what was wrong with what I said, but what else was I supposed to say? Whatever the case was Elder Cooley snapped on me.

"You better be glad you're pregnant because I would've knocked you out of that chair! With your smart mouth, 'I'm gonna take care of it!' "

But what was I supposed to say? I didn't even say it in a nasty way, and even if I did, the point I was trying to make was that I was living in a house with a man who hated me and who was out to get me. I had already revealed how he tried to touch my breast so any little thing I said or did was bad because I was his target.

After our meeting I went to school every day as normal. At that time I was being mistreated by a prejudice teacher who bought and smoked weed from the high school students. I was getting all A's in my other classes but this one teacher gave me an F on my interim report card. I told my mother about the guy and she came up to the school to see what was going on. She had already known he was a jerk and she wanted to see if he was really giving me a hard time.

So one day I came into the classroom and he just told me to "Get out!" I wasn't late or anything so I just looked at him like, *I'm not going nowhere* then I sat down in my chair.

"I told you once and I'm not going to tell you no more!" Everybody in the class was like, *damn, what did she do?* I hadn't given the man any problems or anything. I wasn't getting crunk in the class or nothing. I took my math book out like, *this motherfucker don't tell me to get out. This is where I'm supposed to be this class period.*

"Get out!"

"No."

"I'm going to write you up! I don't want you in my classroom!"

I was pissed at that point because he was just picking on me. So I got up and walked over to his desk.

"You know what, I'm getting out. But before I go, write on my referral that I called you a **BITCH!** 'Cause that's what you is, you a motherfucking **BITCH!** You ignorant ass motherfucker, you probably can't even spell the shit!"

I cussed his ass out and was wrong about it. Disrespecting my elders was something I didn't do but I didn't give a fuck at the time. Then when he gave me my referral I ripped it up and threw it. Everybody started hollering, clapping, banging on the desks yelling, "Whooo whooo whooo! Biancaaaa! As I walked out of the class I heard them say, "I told you she a church girl! She ain't wit dat shit!"

By the time I got home the school had called and left the situation on the answering machine for my mother to hear. Elder Cooley heard it first and by him hearing it first, God forbid what happened to me.

"Bianca, did you call your teacher a bitch and tell him to make sure he spell it right?" he asked me soon as I walked through the door.

"Yes Sir," I answered.

"Why?" I started to tell him why but he cut me off. "You know what? I don't even wanna hear it damn-it! You don't be out to that school talking to those teachers any kind of way! I'm gonna whup your behind before your Mama gets

50

here because I know she ain't gonna want me to whup you because you're pregnant! But as far as I'm concerned, I don't give a damn about you, or that baby! You can fuckin' lose it for all I care! Go get in a slip! Come out your clothes, get naked and get in a slip!"...so he can beat me while I was pregnant.

I didn't even know that what he was doing he could've went to jail for, beating me while I was pregnant. But when I changed into my slip he just beat me and beat me, whupped me and whupped me, and I was pregnant... We had sat there and had a meeting with Garry and everything, but he still beat me... He beat me so bad to where I felt a pull in my stomach that hurt so bad till it made me fall on the floor. When I hit the floor, blood started running down my legs.

While I was on the floor he took the belt that was wrapped around his hand and wrapped it in the opposite direction exposing the buckle. At that time he couldn't see the blood so he told me to "Get up!" When I got up he swung the belt and hit me dead in my eye with the buckle. That was my first black eye ever.

I ended up at the hospital that night then I had a miscarriage and lost the baby that same night. Fresh bruises were all over my body because I was severely beaten not too long ago.

"Honey who did this to you?" all the nurses asked. So I didn't talk to anybody instead I just turned over on my stomach, laid there and cried. I knew if I talked they were going to come and take my mother's kids away from her so I didn't talk so she could keep her kids.

Every time somebody came into the room they asked me who did that to me. One nurse would go and get another nurse, "Look at this," they said while showing the bruises on my back, arms, and legs, plus my black eye. One of them even had tears in her eyes but they didn't roll down.

"Honey, we want to help you but if you don't talk to us we can't help you," the teary eyed nurse explained. "Just tell us who did this to you."

I kept having asthma attacks so they had to keep giving me breathing treatments, but I never told.

After I got home from the hospital I told Bishop Ross about how he made me get into a slip and then beat me.

"He did what?" Bishop Ross asked.

"He made me get in a slip and he beat me," I explained.

"Tell him to call me as soon as he gets home. As old as you are he don't have no business making you get naked and putting you in a slip so he can whup you." Even he didn't understand, making me take off my bra and panties then put me in a slip to beat me?

Like my grandmother told me, he was just mad because I wouldn't fuck him, because I wouldn't stay quiet.

Elder Cooley ended up talking to Bishop Ross about the situation and of course I didn't know what was said. But it couldn't have been too much said because the beatings didn't stop.

One time Elder Cooley over heard me on the phone with a guy name Keith and he thought I was telling him about how he beat me. So he rushed into the room and made me get off the phone.

Chapter 4

I'm Not Taking It!

Another situation was at church during a night service while I was sitting by two of my girlfriends. Elder Cooley tapped one of my friends on her shoulder who was behind me and told her to get my attention. So she got my attention and when I looked over at him he told me to stop clapping off beat. I was like, *off beat? This is how we clap in church. I don't know nothing else.* Then right there in church with every seat in the church filled with church people, Elder Cooley walked up and slapped me in my face while service was going on. "Pooow!"

Prior to that I had been telling my friend Mary about the abuse that was going on and she told me, "The only way he's going to stop beating on you, your mother and your little brother is when y'all start fighting him back. You gotta start fighting him back to let him know you ain't scared of him. I know you're not scared of him, and his problem is he knows you're not scared of him."

So after he slapped me I started fighting him right in the church. When we started fighting service had completely stopped. He tried to pick me up and take me outside as I continually tried to punch him with all the strength I had in me. At that point I was tired, had enough and couldn't take it anymore. So I fought him all the way outside.

When we got home he tried to whup me so we both fought head up like two men in the street. I was throwing stuff at him trying to kill his ass. My mother had to jump between us and beg us to stop. I didn't want to push or hit my mother because I love her, but somebody was about to see that I wasn't going to take that shit anymore and I meant it!

"You better get her!" he yelled while my mother was in the middle of us. "You stupid bitch!" was what he called me.

"Whatever!" I yelled back at him. "That's what I am, whatever!"

I was talking back and fighting like I never done before, because I felt like he was out to get me. I no longer gave a care about him being a Pastor at the Pentecostal Church of God. I had absolutely no respect for him and saw him as just another nigga who was out to get me. He was my enemy at that point, so while my mother was between us I looked him in his face and made sure he understood me.

"You want everybody in this house to be scared of you but I'm not and you know it!" My mother was still between us then all of a sudden he just walked away.

"I want her out of my house," he said as he walked away.

"You want me out of your house? Then I'm gone!" But my mother wouldn't let me go anywhere.

I realized that he was no longer trying to chastise me but he was straight up trying to abuse me. I would've never disrespected any adult like that but he was straight up abusing me, and not only me, but my mother and brother also. He beat my mother till she became senseless. She's not even in her right frame of mind to this day.

But that day he revealed himself to the church again and everybody was saying, "That wasn't necessary, what did she do? She wasn't even doing anything. He just went over and slapped her with all his might!" But did anybody try to help me? Hell no! He hated me and I didn't give a damn because I hated him too. Put two people together who hate each other and you got yourself a war. He started the war but

I was going to end it and I wasn't going out like a punk either. From that day on I fought him every time he tried to whup me. It got to the point where my mother was in the middle of us refereeing.

"I want her out of my house!" was what he said from then on.

"Why you want me out the house? Because I'm standing up for myself and didn't turn out to be a coward or a punk bitch like you tried to make me?"

From then on, every time he approached me with something I didn't like, we just duked it out. Then I started isolating myself and stayed in my room whenever they would go to church events like picnics. They were always going to church members houses to talk and eat but I never went.

At that point I really didn't know who I was. All I knew was I became something that I had been raised not to be. I was raised to be respectful to my elders and Pastors, but I had lost that. Everybody told me I was wrong and should've never started fighting Elder Cooley because he was an adult.

"He's a man and you're a little girl and you need to stay in a little girl's place!" And I would've stayed in my place if I was dealing with a real man.

A little while later Elder Cooley went to see Bishop Ross about the situation that went down between us at church. It was at our next big church meeting when Bishop Ross took his Pastor position away from him.

"If you can't control your own household then how can you tell the people of God what to do?" Bishop Ross said right in the pulpit, which was true.

I was happy he lost his position and on our way home from church that Sunday nobody said anything. The inside of the car was totally silent all the way home. But I was happy, just as long as he didn't touch me and if so, then we were going to go head to head. I had been through too much shit at that point and in-between everything I ran away from home twice.

One time I ran away with Mary at six o'clock in the morning. I faked like I was going to wait on my school bus, but when Mary came we hitch hiked us a ride with some middle aged white guy who drove by.

When we got in his car he asked us if we wanted something to drink and we were like, "Yeah!" He pulled up at a 7-11 and while he was inside I noticed he had some rolled up plastic with some blood on it, a rope, and a machete sticking out from under his seat.

"Mary, look at this stuff he got under his back seat."

"What the hell? Bianca, don't touch it he might be crazy or something let's get out of here!"

We instantly tried to open our doors to get out but neither of our doors would open. I thought my door was locked so I tried to pull the lock up but the lock was gone. That's when we started to panic.

"I can't get out! Mary, open your door!"

"My door won't open either!"

Mary finally decided to crawl out of the driver's door and I hopped over the seat and did the same. We were running down the street when the guy came out of the store yelling, "Hey, where ya'll going?" Then he jumped in his car and started chasing us. "Where y'all going? You little bitches get back here!"

We ended up running into the house of a friend of Mary's. After we explained what happened to the mother of Mary's friend she just looked at us like we were crazy.

"The two of you need to take y'all asses home!" she told us. "You little heifers, y'all think y'all grown! You can get killed out here and it ain't nothing but the grace of God that kept y'all!"

So I called Sister Greer and told her about it. Sister Greer and I were tight at the time and I had spent the night at her house and did her hair on many occasions. She asked me to call her back after a few minutes and when I did she had called Bishop Ross and told him about my situation.

"I called Bishop Ross and he said for you to go home," she told me.

I couldn't believe she called Bishop Ross. What I told her was supposed to be between me and her so I felt like she had betrayed me. But I went home anyway and when I got there my mother and them were screaming, "Where have you been!" Then my mother whupped me and this was the first whuppin' I could ever remember my mother giving me.

"I want you to know I'm not whuppin' you because I want to. I'm whuppin' you because Bishop Ross told me to tell you that you're getting a whuppin' because he said so and it's not for running away!" They understood why I ran away and I guess Bishop Ross opened their eyes to that. "He told me to whup your behind for hitch hiking!"

And not only did he tell her to whup me for hitch hiking, but he also told her to whup me until she got tired.

When Bishop Ross and the other two Bishops of the Pentecostal Church of God say something, the people in the church take it very seriously. So she literally whupped me until she got fucking tired! I was having asthma attacks while she was whuppin' me and everything. I had to take a breathing treatment then go back and get my ass whupped some more.

She whupped me for so long that she had to sit down and drink a can of Coca Cola like she was working or something. I couldn't even accept Bishop Ross for a long time after that because he told my mother to whup me until she got tired and she took heed and did it like a fool. I think he may have said it as a figure of speech but for people in our church when Bishop Ross says something they do it. If he had said for her to kill me, she probably would've killed me. That's how much they believe in what the man says and that's crazy.

♫ ♫ ♫ ♫ ♫

One day I guess my mother couldn't take it anymore because she all of a sudden flipped out on me. There were some guys from my high school who came to our house for me, and the only reason they came over was so I could tell them where another girl we knew lived. All of the guys looked really thugged out with dreadlocks flying all over the place, gold teeth and no shirts on. When they knocked on the door my mother started to flip out.

"Who y'all want?" she asked.

"Is Bianca home?" they asked her.

"Bianca, you got these damn niggas out here in my yard!" she yelled embarrassing me.

"Where Erica stay at?" they asked when I came to the door.

"She that house right there," I pointed.

My mother was upset because she and Elder Cooley had been fighting and for the first time she took her anger out on me.

"What, you fuckin' those niggas? You fuckin' all those niggas?"

"Mama, no I'm not."

"You think you grown?" she yelled just before she charged at me. "What, you wanna hit me? You wanna fight me?'

"Mama no!" I answered while she was in some kind of rage or something.

She charged at me full force like a bull or something from the living-room to my bedroom where I was standing. She had me on my bed then started punching me over and over again in my stomach to the point where I couldn't breathe. Somehow I managed to push her off of me and she fell on the floor. I got on top of her, held her hands down then started screaming.

"You think I wanna fight you?"

"Hit me Bianca hit me, that's what you wanna do, hit me! That's what you want, you wanna beat on me!"

"Mama no, Mama stop!"

"You wanna fight me? Go ahead hit me!"

"Mama what's wrong with you? I don't wanna fight you, I love you!" Then I just got up and walked away.

"Bianca I'm sorry," my mother cried. "I'm sorry Bianca!"

I just threw my hands in the air like, *not you too! You live in this house with me and see what this man do to us and you're about to make me fight you too?* She kept walking through the house following behind me apologizing.

"Bianca wait, wait, wait. Are you mad at me?

"No Mama I'm not mad at you."

"You want some money? Here, take some money."

"No Mama that's okay I got some money." Then she started pulling out her credit cards and that's when I knew something was really wrong with her.

Now that I look back on it, I realize it wasn't me who she was doing it to. It was because he had her mind so messed up and what she wanted to do to him she was doing to me. I guess I was just convenient for her at the time because the stuff she was saying to me didn't make any sense. It was like she couldn't take it anymore and I was feeling it. I guess from him beating on her she felt like that's all everybody wanted to do to her. She took his shit for so many years till that's all she knew.

♫ ♫ ♫ ♫ ♫

I started fighting a lot in high school because all of my life I've been around violence. I ended up getting kicked out of my high school for hitting my teacher in the face with a board in shop class, plus he called me a nigger. After that I went to the Alternative Learning Center (ALC).

ALC was when regular school didn't work out for you that was your alternative. It was a school where they sent kids who were on probation or were pregnant. There were extra security and police officers patrolling the premises. The fence around the school was made like a prison fence because we were considered dangerous kids.

ALC was where I met my boyfriend Keith but at the same time I was still dating my other boyfriend Garry. Eventually I found out Keith was dealing drugs and because of that I broke up with him. At that age, drugs were like so bad to me and I didn't associate myself with anybody who had anything to do with them. But before I had broken up with Keith there was a time when I showed him how to sneak into our house through a broken window in our bathroom.

I'd sneak him into our house all of the time and we'd be straight up having sex. After I broke up with that fool there was a time when I woke up in the middle of the night and he was standing over my bed completely naked. So I had to sit up there and have sex with him and didn't even want to. And that happened over and over until I got pregnant.

Chapter 5

Sean

Not long after I had gotten pregnant I met a young man at church name Sean. He was from Detroit and we saw each other every six months when our church had its big conventions. In June our church has a convention that lasts for two weeks in Detroit, Michigan and in December we have another convention that lasts for one week in Winter Haven, Florida. So we were basically raised up together seeing each other every six months.

Sean used to send me money when I needed it, sometimes his whole pay check. He was also the first person who I told I was pregnant. He'd been trying to get me to go out with him every since that previous convention before I got pregnant but I wouldn't.

Whenever we went to the convention my friends and I would have a bet to see who could get the most phone numbers from all of the different out of town guys. And that's what we went to the convention for, to see who could get the most telephone numbers from the different guys throughout the South and Mid West. Of course I won the bet but that's how I started dating Sean.

The tripped out thing about it was I had Sean's number and I also had his brother Christopher's number. I didn't know they were brothers because they looked like night and day. Christopher is jet black and Sean is yellow looking. With them looking like night and day how was I supposed to know they were brothers? But I never really liked his brother because whenever we would talk I could sense a really strong gay spirit in him. Sean on the other hand, I really liked him. Good thing a friend of mine pulled me aside one day and let me know what was going on. "What are you doing, don't you know they are brothers?" my friend warned me.

After that I only communicated with Sean. Even though he was really skinny and poor looking he was really nice to me. His personality was so sweet. Every day he would save me a seat right next to him in service and even though I didn't want to sit next to him I did it anyway because I didn't want to diss him. I was really trying to give him a chance but he was sweating me really hard.

On the last day of the convention we were getting ready to leave when Sean asked me, "Stand right here. Promise me you're not going to leave until I come back." So I promised and as soon as he took off around the corner I took off and got in the car with my mother and Elder Cooley. When Sean saw us driving down the street headed to I 75 South he ran behind our car trying to stop us.

"Bye Sean!" I opened the door and yelled." I think that was the meanest thing I had ever done to Sean because he was a really sweet guy.

Back in Florida, I talked to Sean off and on and I was really starting to dig him. He was aware that I had a lot of guys who liked me and he was also aware of my baby daddy Keith. I remember when I told him I was pregnant. It was during the church convention in December. Sean was sharing a room with his friends at the Howard Johnson Hotel. That's where we stood in the hallway and talked about our relationship.

"Why Bianca, why won't you be my girl?" he asked me. He sounded so funny to me because Mid Western people tend to sound real proper like Tito and Michael Jackson. They just don't have that country slang like us country folks.

"I can't Sean."

"Why not?"

"Look at my stomach," then he put his hand on my stomach.

"Oh my God," he said with his mouth wide open.

"I'm pregnant, well at least I think I'm pregnant. I almost know I'm pregnant."

"I don't care. I'm in love with you," he told me with both of hands still on my stomach.

"But Sean I'm pregnant."

"I don't care. Are you hungry or anything?"

Little stuff like that made me fall in love with Sean. I was like, *damn, this guy is feeling my stomach and I'm telling him I'm pregnant and he doesn't even care.*

Sean's friends left out of the room so we could be alone. Me and Sean went in and started kissing each other. He always had a hard on for some reason and I was always horny too but I could've waited. But we both got naked anyway, laid on the bed then he put a condom on. He touched my breast and told me I was so beautiful. Then he rubbed my hips with both of his hands.

"Man, do you know how fine you are?"

I had no idea how sexy I was. At that point I was still shy, but not too shy to take control of the situation. That's when I got ready to sit on him and he pushed me off of him.

"This ain't right," he told me.

"Do you want me to lay on back?"

"Yeah, lay on your back."

So I laid on my back then he started kissing my breast. I was nervous because it was our first time together and I got to admit, Sean had the biggest dick that I had seen at that point in my life. I was like, *oh my God* when I saw the condom with his dick in it coming at me. I thought to myself, *what the fuck? He's gonna bust my pussy open!* But I was feeling really freaky right about then and decided to do him anyway.

Every time he got ready to put it in, he would stop so I got confused.

"What's wrong?" I asked him.

"Nothing," he answered while still hard. Then he did the same thing again.

"Sean what's wrong?"

"Bianca I can't do this."

"Why not?"

"Because you're too good for this."

"What?"

"You're too good for this and I can't mess over you like this."

"Mess over me? What do you mean?"

I was dripping wet and could smell my pussy and perspiration so it was time to fuck. In my mind I was saying, *now you wanna tell me this? I ain't no good? Fuck me please!* I wanted it so bad and I don't think I've ever wanted to have sex with a man that bad. So what he told me really offended me. My self-esteem was already low and I was feeling like the ugliest person in the world. I thought I was too skinny and my hips were too big. I had been taken advantage of, abused and molested, so what little bit of self esteem I had left he took it.

"How the hell can you get me naked in the bed then resist me?"

"It's only because I love you." Right after that we put our cloths back on. "Are you okay?"

"Yeah, I'm okay."

"Are you sure?"

"Yeah I'm fine."

I left the room and as I was walking down the hallway I bumped into a friend of mine named Eddie. So I stopped him to get his take on the situation.

"Eddie, you're a man, tell me what you think about this. Sean just had me in the room and we were naked, he put a condom on, the mood was right, he was rubbing and kissing my body, his dick was on hard and everything, but then he stopped. In the middle of everything he just stopped and told me I was too good for that."

I stood there and looked at Eddie then started boo hoo crying.

"Tell me, am I unattractive or something? Am I that ugly? What did I do wrong?"

"Sean really loves you Bianca and everybody can see it. He respects you and cares about you."

The next day Sean and I talked about what happened in-between church services. Back at the hotel I was walking up the stairs in my green and white wrap around skirt as Sean walked behind me holding my hips.

"Your body is like an hour glass," he told me when we took a seat at the top of the stairs. Then he mumbled something that I couldn't understand.

"What did you say Sean?"

"Nothing," he answered as I stood up to re-wrap my skirt.

"Lord just one more time, just one more time," he mumbled again and that time I heard him.

"What do you mean just one more time?"

"If I get one more time," he started beating himself up like he was in regret, "I can't believe I didn't... I'm sorry, but this time I'm ready. I'm going all the way through with it."

We went back into his hotel room to try it again, and all I have to say is **MY LORD, MY LORD, MY LORD!** God smiled on us that day. The sex was good. I wasn't faking my moans or anything because he was really making me moan from deep down inside of me. He gave me the best sex I had ever had at that point in my life.

Sean stood tight by my side that whole convention and we developed a strong bond. From then our six months apart seemed like six years. When he went home he started sending me money for my maternity clothes and anything else I needed for the baby. He was supporting my child when he wasn't even born yet. But the funny thing about this situation was not only was I pregnant, but my mother was pregnant also. My mother and I were straight up pregnant at the same time *(you know you ghetto when)* and for the first time in my life I felt sorry for Elder Cooley. He was living in a house with two pregnant women.

After I started showing and everybody in the church found out I was pregnant, I got put out of the church. They put people out of the church whenever they committed a sin like having sex and getting pregnant. This was forbidden and for that Bishop Ross would stand in the pulpit and announce in front of everybody that you were put out. You could still go to the church and participate but you were not considered an active member and God looked down on you for what you did.

So being put out of the church was devastating. To us it was the worst thing that could happen in the world. So I clung tight to my mother and we were getting along together like peanut butter and jelly. We'd both be in the same bed with our bellies touching and craving Reese's Pieces. I had my son *Little Keith* first then two months later my mother had her daughter, my little sister, and my son's aunt. I went back to church regularly and when they had a "coming home" line I got in it and begged the Lord for forgiveness. After I stood in front of the entire church and told the Lord I was sorry, he then forgave me and I was back in the church.

♫ ♫ ♫ ♫ ♫

My son and my little sister were raised up together and for a long time people thought they were twins. We'd stroll them around in double strollers and sometimes dress them the same. Little fights still broke out around the house but it seemed like once those babies got there some tension was broken. It was new life and like a beginning, well at least that's how I felt. I guess my parents figured, *well there's nothing else we can do, she already gotten herself pregnant and had a baby.* And that's what they were probably trying to prevent. So they kind of laid off of me after that.

Sean and I still only saw each other every six months but we talked over the phone a lot. And it was over the phone when he asked me to marry him. He Fed X'ed me a heart shaped engagement ring with some cubic zirconias around the top of it. I was swept off my feet when I got the ring so the next church convention in Detroit I made sure I had my own hotel room.

I rode to Detroit with my mother and Elder Cooley. Soon as we got there I gave my son to my aunt to care for him while I planned to have myself a ball. And a ball I had, but three days after we arrived in Detroit my mother and Elder Cooley just up'ed and went back to Florida, leaving me stranded in Detroit.

Before I realized they had left me, they were arguing and fighting about the house we were living in back in Florida. I guess they were being evicted and had to hurry up and get back home or something. A lot of times we would use all of our money to go to our church convention even though we couldn't afford it. But our Bishop always told us, "The Lord will provide a way."

I was later told by someone the reason they left me was because I thought I was grown so they were going to treat me like I was grown. Whatever the case was, the fact is they left me stranded in Detroit, Michigan and went back to Fort Meyers, Florida. That's the kind of shit I had to deal with. How are they going to leave a child in another state like that? They took all the other kids but left me. I had no money or food and thank God for Sean because he really took care of me. He fed me breakfast, lunch and dinner every single day and even gave me some money.

I stayed in Detroit for the rest of the convention then ended up catching a ride back to Florida with my Aunt who lived in Jacksonville, Florida. About a month after I was back home in Fort Meyers I found out I was pregnant by Sean. Nine months later I had our daughter L'Tisha and in-between that time I got put out of the church again.

After I had our daughter, Elder Cooley started making a big deal about me and my kids living in his house.

"I pay the bills here! I bring the food in here!" were some of the things he made a big deal about. As usual, he tried to make me feel like I wasn't shit. I wasn't shit and as far as he was concerned I wasn't going to be nothing but shit, if that.

One day my mother was telling her kids what to eat before she went to work.

"Y'all can get some cereal but don't eat up those babies WIC cereal because those babies gotta eat. Y'all can go to school and eat if it's not enough." So I said something to my little brother Derrick in the way of don't eat that box of Cheerios because I bought that with my WIC check.

"And next time don't go and eat up all the cereal in the house then turn around and eat my baby's cereal! Mama already told y'all not to do that!"

As I was talking to Derrick, Elder Cooley flipped out on me.

"This is my house you don't tell nobody what to eat in here!" Elder Cooley yelled. "I don't care if you did bring it in here! You don't pay a damn dime on nothing in here! You ain't nothing but a hoe!"

"Whatever," I smartly replied, "whatever!"

"I want you out of my house you damn hoe! Get out of my house!"

"You ain't said nothing," I told him then went and started packing me and my kids bags. Right after that I left.

I went down the street to a friend's house and explained what happened to her and her mother. After I finished explaining their response was, "What? That's a damn shame. He's been wanting to put you out every since day one! You can stay here for as long as you need to get yourself together."

I bounced from house to house for a while until finally I ended up going to Jacksonville, Florida and staying with my Aunt Donna. Sean came to Jacksonville to be with me and our child and we all stayed at Aunt Donna's house together. We planned to get married and start a new life in Florida so Sean started looking for work. Three months later Sean still had no work and that's when he started to realize Florida wasn't where he wanted his home to be. He became sad and depressed and told me he missed his family back home. So after three months Sean went back to Detroit.

I ended up leaving Florida and went to Detroit to start a life with Sean and the kids. My kids and I stayed with a friend of mine from our church name Arketa Gordon. Arketa was living with her mother at the time but her mother gladly welcomed me and my kids. Sean was still out of work but he said he had something lined up plus somebody from the church was going to let us rent one of their homes.

Not long after I arrived in Detroit Sean took me to church because he made an appointment for us to talk to the head Bishop there named Bishop Duren. When we took our seats in Bishop Duren's office, Sean told him he wanted to marry me.

"So y'all trying to be in love?" Bishop Duren asked us.

"Yes Sir," we both answered.

"That's good, that's the way the Lord wants it," he said nodding his head.

Bishop Duren gave us his blessing and permitted us to get married. I was so happy when we left out of his office because I felt like Sean had just rescued me from a horrible life. He was my knight in shining armor.

Chapter 6

Exhale

I went back to Florida to tell my mother how Bishop Duren had told us we could get married, plus to get the rest of my belongings. A day before I was to leave Florida for the last time I got a call from Sean's sister-in-law Wanda, who was also a member of our church.

"Every time I see Sean, I see Arketa," Wanda explained. "Are you and him still together, because I just want to know?"

"Yes, me and Sean are still together."

"Are you sure? Because every time I see him, he's with Arketa. She be riding in the front seat of his car and they be off into their own little world in the back of the church. Sunday at church I was coming out of the kitchen on my way up the stairs and they were on the stairway talking. I'm not trying to start nothing but I just thought you should know."

After that I called Sean and asked him about it.

"Sean, be honest with me and tell me what's going on. Is there somebody else? If you don't want to be with me then you need to let me know. Let's not make a mistake that we'll both regret."

"What are you talking about?" he asked me.

"I heard you're messing around with Arketa."

"Me and Arketa been friends for years. It's nothing."

"Okay, well if you don't want to be honest with me then I'm going to call Arketa and ask her myself."

So I called Arketa to see if she was going to say something about it but she didn't. I talked to Sean about it again and he demanded that I tell him where I had heard the rumor."

"Who told you this because somebody's hatin' on me and don't want to see us together?" I told him it wasn't important who told me then I let the situation go. But then I got a call from Arketa and she was confessing.

"I'm sorry about what's going on," she told me, "but Sean needs to be the one to tell you what happened."

"What happened," I asked becoming instantly pissed off.

She didn't tell me what happened and told me I needed to talk to Sean. But fuck Sean! I just not too long ago had that man's baby, my parents were flipping out on me because of it, plus I thought I had a future with Sean. As for Arketa, that slimy bitch! We were supposed to be real tight but all along she was trying to take my man. I guess all the years we've been friends didn't mean nothing to her. So I called Sean back.

"She already called me and told me what was going on. I just want you to confirm it and tell me the truth. Don't lie to me!"

He came out and told me they just kissed and that was that.

"Do you want to be with her?" I asked him. "If you want to be with her just tell me and I won't even come back to Detroit. I'll let it be what it is."

"No Bianca, I love you. I'm sorry this should've never happened."

I was so upset about what happened I had to call Bishop Ross and talk to him about it. After I told him what happened he told me everybody makes mistakes and we need to learn to forgive people. Then we came to the conclusion that it was only a kiss so I forgave Sean and went back to Detroit.

I was so happy to be there and we were in love all over again. We stayed with Wanda and Sean's brother until we were able to move into our own house. Wanda was a real cool chick. A lot of people tried to poison me by telling me how she was a snake but she made us feel very welcome in their home.

It wasn't long after I arrived in Detroit that I had seen snow for the very first time in my life. Sean and I were coming out of a CVS drug store and I was trying to hurry back to the car because it was unbelievably cold. As Sean was placing the kids in the car he was talking to me at the same time. Then I felt something wet hit my nose. I thought he had accidentally spit on me but then it happened again and he wasn't even facing me.

"Something just fell on me," I told Sean.

"That's snow baby," he came over and hugged me. "This is your first snow experience."

"Oh my God, I thought you were spitting on me," I laughed.

Whenever it would snow, I would take my kids outside and we'd make snow angels in the front yard. To me, the snow was the most beautiful thing I had ever seen.

After two weeks me, Sean, and the kids moved into a house on the Westside of Detroit. The street was called Northlawn and we rented the house from a member of our church. We weren't married yet so us living together with my two kids was a big problem for his family and a lot of church members. A lot of self-righteous people were saying we were just shacking and shouldn't be living like that.

But I loved our new home. It was a big house with two bedrooms on the first floor, three bedrooms upstairs and a basement. We didn't have much when we started out because Sean didn't have a job. But he eventually landed a job at Boston Market and saved up enough money to upgrade his 1987 Escort to a 1997 Escort and we were doing okay. We were happy about having our own place and new wheels but we were still poor.

We had a TV you turned with knobs that was sitting in a chair. We didn't have any furniture at the time but it didn't matter because we had each other. It wasn't long after that when Sean hooked up with some people who gave us some furniture and that was a blessing in itself. They gave us a queen size bed, a car bed for my son Little Keith and a baby crib for our daughter L'Tisha.

Everything was perfect. There was no arguing, fighting, or anything of the sort. After a while Sean landed a better job with a company called RIMCO so I had to adjust to staying in that big house while he worked longer hours. But I was still happy. I was like, *wow, I got my own life here. I don't have nobody trying to beat on me and I don't have to live in a domestic violent environment.* I was finally able to exhale... at least that's what I thought.

Chapter 7

I'z Married Now

One evening Sean came in from work and soon as he hit the door he had his pants halfway down while we were kissing and moaning, "Umm, um, yes baby!" That's how we were with each other. We were some passionate love making people. We loved to make love to each other and we were having sex like crazy all over the house. Soon as he'd hit the door, the kids would be asleep, dinner would be on the table and he wouldn't even be out of his work clothes good before we would go at it.

We made it to the bedroom where he laid me on the bed. I was completely naked and had my hand in my pussy while playing with my clit. Sean took his pants off then unbuttoned his shirt before he laid on top of me. Then the phone rang. "Hello," he reached over and answered. "Who is this?" he asked the caller as I rubbed my feet on his dick. "Oh, praise the Lord Bishop Duren!"

Sean quickly started putting his pants back on like Bishop Duren had straight up walked into his own room and caught us fucking in his bed. He pulled and zipped up his pants while scared to death of what we were about to do. I just looked at him like, *Bishop Duren can't see you!!* He was actually so scared that he tucked his work shirt back into his pants. It's crazy as hell that those men *(the Bishops)* have that kind of power over people.

Bishop Duren called to ask Sean when were we getting married?

"Soon Bishop," Sean explained. "We already went downtown to see about getting the marriage license and it was so many people there but we were helped anyway and now it won't be long."

Bishop Duren told Sean he understood but we needed to hurry up and do what we needed to do. Right then I knew people were in our business and telling it back to Bishop Duren. One of the people I knew was in our business was Sean's grandmother. She didn't like me and didn't want Sean to be with me. Plus by me being put out of the church, a lot of people felt like no one should deal with me until I got back in.

A week later we got married and I guess since I was married I was officially back in the church and an active member of the Pentecostal Church of God. It was a cold day in February when we had our very small wedding at our church, the Pentecostal Church of God. I really didn't want a wedding, instead I wanted to simply go into Bishop Duren's office and let him marry us. But we had a ceremony anyway because two of Sean's brothers talked him into it.

It was a normal wedding but I had no family support. Not one person in my family was there, not even my mother. Three of Sean's family members came to support us *(Wanda, her husband and Christopher)*. Christopher even got on the organ and played "Here Comes the Bride." Our pastor Elder Strong married us and there was an additional five church members who came to our wedding to show us some support.

A lot of Sean's family claimed he didn't tell them about the wedding but Sean said he did. I guess our wedding wasn't a big deal to them. But I wasn't surprised because they acted as if they never liked me anyway. For some reason they thought I was a whore and Sean was making a big mistake by marrying me. But we got married anyway and were happy with our small ceremony. And even though we were the newlyweds, Sean and I treated the few people at our wedding out to the Olive Garden.

There was an older couple at the Olive Garden who sent a waitress over to our table to ask Sean a question.

"The gentleman over there wants to know if it would be okay if he bought your table a bottle of champagne. He said your wife is the most beautiful bride he's seen in a long time."

It was a nice compliment from the strange old white man who bought us a bottle of champagne. When the wine was brought to us he and his wife clapped their hands. As they were leaving they came over and kissed me on my cheek.

"You look like a princess, you're so beautiful," the wife told me.

When Sean and I got home we made a pallet on the living-room floor. We had our champagne bottle that we brought home from the restaurant, two bottles of wine that we picked up from the store, some cake and a few other desserts we brought home from the restaurant. Our night was magical and the most romantic night I had ever had.

Two days later I heard a knock on the door while I was in the bathroom. I rushed to the door as quickly as I could only to find Arketa getting back into her car and driving down the street. I called her later on that evening and she told me she was sorry about what happened between her and Sean. She also told me she felt like she owed me an apology.

"What are you talking about Arketa?" I asked confusingly. "He told me the only thing that happened was a kiss."

"Is that what he told you?" she asked me.

"Yes!"

"Oh. Is that really all he told you?"

"Arketa did something else happen?" I asked angrily because the situation was starting to hit me hard. We were only married for two days and still had the champagne and wine bottles laying around. "Arketa you know that's fucked up! You're supposed to be my friend! You got the nerves to call me two days after we got married and bring this up! Why didn't you tell me before? This is some fucked up shit!"

I was in a rage because in so many words she told me she and Sean had fucked. Later on, when Sean walked in the house I fussed at him about it then we got into a big argument. I was in his face telling him how he wasn't shit and then he shoved me into the stairs. I got up and shoved him back then we started straight up fighting.

As we were fighting Sean picked up the champagne bottle the old man bought us and he busted it across my head. I fell to the floor feeling like I was about to lose consciousness. Then I got up and realized my forehead was busted open as the blood rolled down my face.

There I was again feeling like shit thinking to myself, *damn, I got put out of my house, I've left Florida and now I'm in a house where I have to fight my own husband. I can't win for losing, what kind of fucked up shit is this?* That's when I got my kids, put them in the double stroller and we started walking down the snow covered streets.

Before I left the house I called Wanda and told her I would be walking down 7 Mile Rd. and to come pick me up because Sean and I had gotten into it. As cold as it was outside, I was walking around with my kids while holding a towel with some ice in it on my forehead. There was a big knot on my forehead and it seemed to swell larger by the minute.

When Wanda finally pulled up she parked along side of the road then got out to help us in.

"What the hell happened to you?" she asked when she saw the big knot on my head. "Hell naw, Sean needs his ass kicked!"

"Wanda don't tell nobody about this," I pleaded. "Just take me to your house."

Sean ended up calling Wanda's house to apologize and he told me he was trying to hit the bottle against the wall. For some reason I believed him so me and the kids went back home. Even though I went back to Sean I was still homesick and wanted to go back to Florida. But I couldn't go back because of the situation when Elder Cooley put me out. I didn't even feel like I could call my mother and tell her about what I had gone through two days after my wedding. That's when I started feeling like I didn't have anybody.

♫ ♫ ♫ ♫ ♫

They say if you grow up in a domestic violent home eventually you will have one of your own. And that's what happened in my case.

♫ ♫ ♫ ♫ ♫

Chapter 8

The People Don't Like Me

Our life went on but the situation between Arketa and Sean was still a hard pill for me to swallow. I had given up my life for that man. I had scholarships concerning my music career and I gave it up to get married because I thought he loved me. But now all we do is argue about this Arketa situation.

Eventually the situation died down but my health was starting to give me problems. Wanda took me to a clinic where two doctors practiced, one of which was a man name Dr. Everett Hamrick. Dr. Hamrick was a tall man of African descent but he had a head full of what seemed to be "good hair." He ended up being my primary care physician and I desperately needed him because I had chronic asthma, upper respiratory disease and was having acute asthma attacks.

He took my blood and did a pap smear and everything came back negative with no STD's. He prescribed me some pills to help me with my breathing and I was on my way. Three months later I went back to Dr. Hamrick because I was nauseous, fatigue, had stomach and lower back pain, could barely breathe, plus I had a fever of 103. Come to find out, I was coming down with the flu. Then Dr. Hamrick asked me a question in a low voice.

"Who's the lucky fellow?"

"What do you mean who's the luck fellow?" I asked confusingly.

"You can tell me, I'm your doctor. I'm not going to tell anybody. Who are you cheating with? I remember you told me you just got married and the two of you are cheating already?"

"Dr. Hamrick, I'm not cheating on my husband. What are you talking about?"

"Well, you have a small case of Chlamydia."

"What? What do you mean I have a small case of Chlamydia?"

"I know you have to be cheating because when I did your blood work and pap smear three months ago everything was negative. If you're being honest with me, I'd hate to be the one to tell you but your husband is cheating on you."

I was hurt by what Dr. Hamrick told me. At the time things were going kind of good between me and Sean. Therefore, I didn't want any more arguing or fighting so I didn't say anything to Sean about it. I came on him in a different way.

"Sean, will you be honest with me because I want to ask you something?" I asked him as we were laying in the bed. "It's not about you and Arketa but honey, are you cheating on me?"

"No," he answered really quickly. "No Bianca."

"Sean are you sure?"

"Yes I'm sure, I promise."

I knew he was lying to me but because I didn't want any more fighting and everything was fine between us, I told him Dr. Hamrick told me I had strep throat and it was contagious. Therefore I needed him to take some antibiotics with me because it wasn't going to do any good if only I took them and he infected me again.

Sean believed me and that's how I got him to take the antibiotics. Later on I went back to my doctor and my STD was gone, but being married was really stressing me out. We were newlyweds and already we were on our second infidelity. I was living in a big city and didn't know too many people. Therefore, I felt all alone because I didn't even have one single family member I could call for help. My mother was totally clueless to what was going on and when she did call me I faked it.

"Yeah Mama everything is good. We're so happy together."

I'm a very private person and plus I felt like if I told her, she and Elder Cooley would've probably been happy and said, "That's what you get for leaving! You should've stayed in Florida!" But either way, I would've been going through the same domestic violence bullshit.

♫ ♫ ♫ ♫ ♫

I spent most of my time in church, going to the hospital for my asthma, and going to see Dr. Hamrick. My asthma kept me really sick because there's a big difference between the weather in Florida and Detroit. My asthma was acting up so bad to where I was going to the hospital almost every three days. The same paramedics would come pick me up almost every time and they knew me by my first name. I went to Sinai Grace Hospital so much that the doctors even knew me by name.

I was under a lot of stress because of my health and the fact that I knew my husband was cheating on me. Whenever he would leave the house I was scared because there was a possibility he was going to cheat on me. Even with that, I still wanted our marriage to work so I prayed and talked to the Lord about the situation. I felt like I didn't have anybody else so the Lord was where my help was coming from. I was going to church on Tuesday and Friday evenings, Sunday morning Bible School, Sunday noon service, Sunday YPU service and Sunday evening service. If there was a special prayer or meeting in between those services I was there also because I wanted my marriage to work. I loved that man and wanted him to love me too.

Because of Arketa and him giving me a STD, I felt like he didn't love me. But he eventually came out and told me the truth about him and Arketa.

"Why didn't you tell me the truth when I was in Florida?" I asked Sean.

"I lied because I was afraid you wouldn't marry me."

"What right do you have to do that? You basically made the decision for me by lying to me."

If he would've told me the truth back then I wouldn't have came back. I would've been a fool to walk into something like that with my eyes wide open.

The only thing I knew to do in order to help us was to get more involved in church. I also sang in the choir thinking it was somehow going to help us but then our marriage started to go even more downhill.

♫ ♫ ♫ ♫ ♫

Summer had rolled around and our church convention had just ended. Sean had been spending a lot of time with his old girlfriend from our church named Dawn Davison. Dawn had moved down South but stayed in Detroit after the convention to spend some time with her family. One day I was walking through the house and I saw Sean on the phone. When he saw me he slammed the phone down and walked away so fast that you could say he was running.

"Sean, who were you talking to?" I asked, fearing he was cheating on me.

"I was talking to Dawn," he answered embarrassedly.

"Why would you be sneaking and talking to her? What's going on? Are you fucking her too?"

"I just wanted to call her and spend some time with her while she was in town."

"Okay, do you want me spending time with my ex? How would you feel if I called Garry and asked him did he want to hook up?"

Dawn and her family were some of the people who caused a lot of problems in our marriage, basically her mother and some of the people they hung around. As far as going to church, Dawn's mother made it real hard for me because she stayed in our business. We were supposed to be the "people of God" and they were behaving more like the people of the Devil.

One Sunday after service Dawn's mother was sitting in the basement. Sean and I were headed to our car and I had L'Tisha in my arm plus Little Keith by his hand. As we walked pass Dawn's mother she stopped Sean so I stopped also because he tapped me.

"No, I don't want her, I just want to talk to you," she bust out and told Sean.

"Stay right there Bianca," was what he told me.

"We're having a dinner at our house and I want you to know you're invited, and just you only," she told Sean.

How rude and disrespectful she was and that's just the kind of treatment I got from people at the Detroit church. I was standing right there when she said it so I threw my hand up like *whatever* then walked away with my kids.

"Bianca, Bianca," Sean pleaded as I walked away. It seemed like every time I went to church there was something new with that Davison family. I think it was all because Dawn didn't like me because she felt like I broke up their little fling or whatever they had going on. But they gave me a lot of hell and that hurt me.

Looking back on it I have to ask myself, "Why would I let that affect me?" I was so into church and I thought the people there were supposed to be kind and loving. Dawn's mother was over fifty years old and I couldn't understand why she would be acting so childish, especially towards young people.

It began to be too stressful for me to go to church because they would always do something to hurt my feelings. They were just a bunch of females who were jealous of me and I had to deal with it at church out of all places. Then one day Sean called Dawn and she called him back. I answered the phone and felt so humiliated after I hung up on her. The situation bothered me so much till Sean and I had to go and talk to Bishop Duren about it, for the second time.

"Sean and I have been in here before and talked to you about these same people," I explained to Bishop as I told him what the Davison family did. "When we come to church they'll speak to him and won't even speak to me. They hug and kiss all on him and won't have nothing to say to me."

"If they can't speak to your wife then you don't speak to them," Bishop Duren told Sean.

They were making it so hard for me to be a new member of the Pentecostal Church of God in Detroit. Sean eventually apologized to me in Bishop Duren's office for the hell he was making in our home.

"How would you feel if a man came up to me and hugged and kissed all over me and didn't say anything to you?" I asked Sean. But most of the time men don't do stupid shit like that. It was a female thing I was dealing with. And even after what was said in the office nothing changed so we started having fights and getting physical about the situation.

One Sunday we had a fight because I walked up and saw Arketa and Sean hugging and talking after church. Soon as I walked up she walked away and didn't say anything to me.

"I'm your wife and I feel so disrespected," I yelled at Sean. "Especially when this is the same bitch that caused us so many problems!" When we got home we started fighting. It seemed like every time we went to church, we came home and fought about him and another woman, or the Davison family.

One day Dawn's sister Tiff was outside the church talking to Sean and when I walked up she just walked away.

"Don't be like that," Sean told Tiff.

"Let her be how she wanna be!" I yelled at Sean. "I'm going to the car!"

"Bianca, Bianca, don't go nowhere!" He was talking to me so rudely that it seemed like he was trying to embarrass me in front of her. So we argued about it all the way home.

When we got in the house we physically fought about it and this was one time when he straight up started choking the shit out of me. After he finished choking me he put a blue laundry basket over my head, started jerking it back and forth with my head in it, and held me down with his knee in my back the whole time.

After the fight he went in one room and I went into another. We eventually ended up in the same bed before the night was over and the next morning he went to work as usual. I had bruises all over me from the fight and had started getting used to seeing them. When Sean came home from work he apologized and told me our fighting had to stop. I agreed and we promised not to fight each other anymore.

It wasn't long after the telephone situation between Sean and Dawn when I went to church where people were laughing in my face and talking about me like a dog. People would sit right behind me and say, "She's the stupid one. He was just fooling around with Arketa and now he's trying to mess around with me."

I talked to Dawn face to face and when I went to see her at her sisters' house, all five of her sisters were standing on the porch staring at me.

"Dawn, can I talk to you?" I asked standing in the walkway. Dawn came off the porch and seemed to be taking me as a joke.

"Wasn't he just fucking Arketa?" Dawn asked me. "And now he's trying to fuck me too!"

"I don't have a problem with you Dawn, my problem is with him. All I want to know is the truth."

"I don't have a problem with you either but you need to check your man. That nigga is on me. I'm not thinking about him. All he wants is some pussy."

I stood there and cried my eyes out in front of her and it was all a big joke to her. Later I felt like a fool for standing up there and letting her see me cry for what she helped do to my marriage. I should've never gone to her in the first place. At church we were told not to hate your Brother or Sister and if you do then you go to them and you work it out. That's how I was raised so I didn't want any problems with anybody. But that family is not the type of people who you can talk to because they live for drama and confusion. Misery loves company and they are miserable and want everybody else to be miserable with them.

That night Sean and I were up all night arguing about Dawn. When morning came and it was time for him to go to work we were still arguing. He got in the car and as he was backing out of the driveway I ran to the car and hit the windshield with my hand. The windshield cracked when I hit it because that's just how mad I was. I felt like I was getting choked, slapped and beat on all because of some dumb shit he was doing with the people at church. So I ended up calling Bishop Duren at his office.

"Bishop, I don't think I'll ever be the same again," in tears I cried on the phone. "These people are causing so much confusion in my home. I'm getting my head bust and I'm getting bruises all over my body from fighting."

"All of this fighting is something that's happening more and more often," Bishop explained. "They try to say that everybody is doing it, but everybody is not doing it! I'm not doing it and Bishop Ross is not doing it! None of us are doing it! This is a shame!"

"Bishop I don't want the marriage anymore. I give up. I want to go home."

"I know it's rough but I believe you are stronger than that and you'll pull through everything."

Bishop encouraged me to stay strong but after I got off the phone I still wanted to go home. I was feeling really out of place and my support was supposed to be the church but the people at the church were making it harder for me.

After I got off the phone I started having an asthma attack so I went to Dr. Hamrick. When I got there I was so sick he told me I needed to be put on oxygen because my oxygen level was way too low. I was light headed and my toes and fingers were tingling because there wasn't enough oxygen getting to my brain. So he ordered me some oxygen and the next day it arrived at my house.

He also prescribed me a lot of medication and some of which were narcotics. He told me the narcotics would help me relax and sleep better. I was on a sleeping pill called Restoril, a pill called Paxil for my depression, Benadryl 50mg, Tylenol #3 and another pill I could never figure out how to pronounce. After I started taking the medications it was making me sleep a lot. Even though I slept a lot, the arguing between me and Sean had gotten worse.

Then I noticed I started slowing down on the things I did around the house and how I was able to care for my kids. I wasn't cleaning up or cooking because all I wanted to do was sleep all the time. That's how the medications made me feel.

After a while I tried to stop taking the medications because Sean and I wanted to have another baby for some strange reason. Even though our marriage was a lot of lies and cheating on his behalf, we were still trying to get through it. He started to see some of the things people were doing to us and after that he was teaming up with me to make me feel like we were in this thing together. But I was still being deceived because not long after that I found out Sean was messing around with one of Bishop Duren's granddaughters named Crystal Duren.

I found out when I got on our computer one day and read some e-mails they had been sending to each other. They had been writing love letters to each other and had an affair going on for God knows how long. It was like before I could get over one woman Sean had another one. I couldn't even heal from one situation before he put us in another one.

Sean apologized to me and promised he would never do it again. Then he started going back and forth to counseling with Bishop Duren about his cheating, arguing and fighting. Sometimes I went to counseling with him and Bishop Duren told us to stay prayerful and to keep going to church.

I can't say that Sean was a straight monster because we both were young and foolish at the time. Two young people entering into a marriage at a young age can be really stressful. So we tried to work on our problems by talking to each other in order to get to know each other a little better.

Sean was given an active position in the Sunday YPU services for the young people on Sundays. One thing that was really weighing heavy on me was the fact that the same bitch, Crystal Duren worked in the YPU service. And, to make things worse they worked side by side with each other. I told Bishop Duren about this when we went to counseling and once again he told me, "I believe you are stronger than that. I believe you can take it."

I accepted what Bishop told me but it was still hard for me to go to church. Everybody there was already saying, "She's so stupid for staying with him. Sean really doesn't want to be with her, he only married her because she had his baby." But still I was trying to be that church going woman they raised me up to be. Basically, I was trying to be what everybody was telling me I was supposed to be. "A child of God would be this way," they would tell me. "Fight the good fight of faith and hold on," and I was trying to do that. "Press on. Strive on," so that's what I was doing.

It was because of the church why I was married. I wasn't married because I wanted to be. I was married because Bishop Duren was encouraging me to stay in the marriage and try to work it out. So I stayed, then I got pregnant again. When I got pregnant things calmed down and I felt like all of our problems were resolved. We didn't even do too much arguing at that time.

Chapter 9

Davenport

Towards the end of my pregnancy my doctor examined me then told me my placenta was attached to my cervix. Normally the placenta is attached to the stomach wall but mine wasn't. So with that I was expected to die while giving birth. My doctor and some other specialists told me and Sean I needed an emergency c-section and I was not going to live through the birth. The baby was to go home with Sean and he had to care for it because I was not going to live.

"When I cut your stomach open and we remove the baby," the doctor explained, "then I have to remove the placenta. A c-section is already high risk but this will put you at deaths because we have to remove the placenta from your cervix. It can't stay in there, and soon as we remove it the problem will begin. You will start to hemorrhage and then you'll bleed to death."

They scheduled me for an emergency c-section and the date for it was only two weeks away. I'll never forget that date because that's the day they told me I was going to die. I broke down in the doctor's office while wondering who was going to take care of my kids?

"I know you are church people," the doctor told us, "so you need to call your church and have them pray for your situation."

Walking out of the doctor's office I was feeling numb all over. I had never been that scared in my entire life, but little did I know was the Lord had something better planned for me. When the date came and the doctor and hospital staff prepared me for surgery, right there in front of all of us a miracle was preformed. While they were doing the ultra sound to figure out where they were going to cut me, the nurse kept repositioning the camera.

"It's been moved," the nurse told us.

"Thank you Jesus, thank you Jesus!" Sean and I both yelled out."

They didn't believe my placenta had been moved so they rolled my bed over to a bigger ultra sound machine and there they discovered the same thing. The placenta had been moved. They took all of the equipment off of me, sent me home and I didn't have to have my baby early like they planned. I felt like my life was spared, God heard my cry. The Lord had something different planned and I was so thankful for that. He allowed the placenta to move over to the right just enough so I could have a vaginal labor. Not long after that I gave birth to our beautiful daughter Faith.

♫ ♫ ♫ ♫ ♫

One day I had to help Sean and his sister get some FIA assistance for their mother. I wasn't even supposed to be out of the house because I had not too long ago given birth. But Sean and his family acted as if they didn't know anything about the FIA system, so because I was nice I went with them.

At the FIA office Sean, his sister and their mother went into the social worker's office while I sat in the lobby with my kids. They were back there for a long time then the social worker came out of the office without them. She then walked over to me and started talking to my kids and rubbing them on their heads. I thought she was just the average social worker at the time that was just being nice to my kids.

About two months after we went to the FIA office there was a night when Sean and I were getting ready to have sex. When Sean took off his clothes he had dried up pussy cum all over his dick and between his legs. I was hurt out of this world and just went nuts.

"What the fuck is this?" I asked knowing it wasn't from me because we hadn't had sex in three days. I screamed and yelled then went into the bathroom and slammed the door. "Why are you doing this to me? Sean who is it, who is it?"

Later on Sean ended up confessing how he had been seeing a woman named Antoinette Davenport and she just so happened to be same woman who worked at the FIA office on Fullerton.

"Who is Antoinette," I asked Sean.

"Antoinette Davenport," he answered.

"Where do you know her from?"

"I know her from one of the houses I was working on."

"Take me to her! I wanna know who she is!" So Sean took me to her house.

When we got to her house we walked on the porch and Sean knocked on the door.

"Who is it?" she yelled from the other side of the door.

"It's Sean!" Then she looked out of curtains and saw me standing there.

"Oh shit!" she yelled before she opened the door. When she let us in my whole world fell apart. I was crying and everything as I looked into the eyes of the woman he was cheating on me with. I thought everything was okay between me and Sean. We weren't arguing or fighting. We'd just had a new baby and the Lord had spared my life, so I thought everything was okay. But all along he was cheating on me with this woman.

The woman had to be about a size three with short, thin, black hair. She looked just like a man, a crack head man. Looking at her put a question in my mind asking, *is Sean gay?* She didn't have nothing on me. I couldn't even feel intimidated by her because the beauty couldn't compare, even though I had low self-esteem. But even with my low self-esteem I had to ask, *you wanna cheat on me with this? If you want to cheat on me don't go from something good to worse! Go from something good to better! Don't just go and fuck any damn thing!*

After I told Antoinette who I was she started apologizing and told me she was sorry about everything.

"My problem is not with you," I explained to her. "You didn't make a commitment to me, he did. But I just wanted to be aware of who you are to make sure you're not somebody I'm letting come into my home or be around my kids."

When I asked her how long they had been seeing each other, the two of them were trying to get their dates together. They were looking at each other and trying to give eye signals and little crazy shit. But she was lying and he was still lying. Every time I asked a question they gave each other eye signals so I just got up and walked out of the door as Sean followed behind me.

I didn't even get back in the car. Instead I walked down 7 Mile Rd. as Sean slowly drove alongside me with our kids in the back seat.

"Bianca get back in the car," he constantly begged.

"No, just go, I'll walk back to the house just go away."

"Baby I'm sorry, Bianca please I'm sorry!"

I couldn't even call anybody and tell them about the bullshit situation. So I eventually went back home feeling like shit. That same night Sean grabbed me by my ankle and started crying.

"Baby, I'm sorry. I know I fucked up. I fucked it all up! I know it's my fault baby. I'm so sorry. You were doing everything right! Baby it's me!" I'm just a person with a big heart and I forgive everybody who's hurting me. I was taught this when I was a child to hide people like the man who was molesting me.

"No it's not all your fault," I told Sean.

"No, Bianca don't say that. It is my fault! I know you won't ever forgive me, so I'm going to leave right now. I'll go live somewhere else!"

"Sean you don't have to go. I accept your apology." Sean just looked at me then bust out crying even harder.

"I know you want it to be over," he cried.

"No I don't. We've been through all of this other stuff so we can get through this... but you have to help me because I'm hurt right now." We were on the floor in our living-room as I explained, "I don't even know what I'm feeling right now. This is new to me and I have never felt nothing like this. This is a different kind of hurt. It's different from the domestic violence and child abuse. I've been betrayed like a motherfucker!"

It was a hurt I thought I would never be able to get over, let alone write about. Even though he wanted to leave, I wouldn't let him. I was still trying to be that wife and what they taught me to be in that church.

"No baby you don't have to go nowhere. Where are you going to go?"

"I don't know. I don't have nowhere to go."

The next day I got up, went to the payphone and called Bishop Duren about the situation because that's how we were raised. Any problems we had in our house we were to go and talk to the Bishops about it. So I went to Bishop Duren, again.

"Where is he right now?" Bishop asked with authority as I stood at the payphone.

"He's at home," I answered.

"Where are you?"

"I'm at a payphone."

"Tell him I want to see him."

Sean eventually went and talked to Bishop Duren and then there was an appointment made for the both of us to go. When we went Bishop Duren told Sean about himself.

"Man you done messed up," Bishop told Sean. "Look at her! She doesn't deserve that, and she's still by your side! She loves you! Do you love her?"

"Yes Sir," Sean answered.

"I don't think you do! If you love her why would you keep taking her through this?"

Bishop really let Sean know that he had a good wife who stood by his side. "But you just keep hurting her and she's trying to make it work." And I was really trying hard but the reputation I had in the church was, "Bianca is so mean, she's so nasty, she's got an attitude and will flip the script on you in a minute." But nobody had any idea of what I was going through in my house. Everybody was looking at Sean like *oh poor innocent Sean.*

Even though I forgave Sean and told him he didn't have to leave, I still felt so unimportant. Those same words Elder Cooley used towards me as a child came back to haunt me. "You'll never be good for nothing but laying on your back! You'll be a good housewife." I thought to myself, *damn, I'm not even that. I'm not even a good housewife. I must not even be good for laying on my back so I guess I'm nothing.* The depression just slapped me in my face. I was already feeling insecure as hell because he kept cheating on me, and for what I didn't know.

Even though I wanted to, I just couldn't get over the Antoinette Davenport situation and it completely destroyed our marriage. The situation made us start arguing more than we ever argued before. At the time, I was heavily medicated because my health was kind of bad. I started taking more pills then I ever took before, not realizing I was becoming an addict. The pills I was taking really wasn't working so Dr. Hamrick told me to start taking two of everything and if I ran out to come and see him and he would give me some more.

Through all of the drama, my breathing and general health was bad and since I was on narcotics I could only get my prescriptions every thirty days. But I was running out of pills before my thirty days were up. And not only was I having breathing problems and didn't have enough medication to last me, I also had to take care of my three kids. I had the pressure of my husband cheating on me, all the bullshit with the church people, and all of it was having a mental effect on me. Plus my medications clearly stated, "This medication may cause mental confusion, memory loss, sensitivity to sunlight, illusions, delusions, if these symptoms occur follow up with your doctor."

So I was doing what my doctor was telling me to do as far as taking my medication. Then at the same time, my marriage had completely fallen apart. I was sleeping in my kid's room, on the couch, and on the floor so I wouldn't sleep next to him. I felt like I was just all fucked up. My marriage was fucked up, including my head, my mind, my heart, my house and the church. So I was just completely fucked up.

One day I told Bishop Duren I felt like I was never going to be the same again. He told me I probably wouldn't ever be the same again and I just put my head down and started crying.

After that, we started fighting more than ever. I was getting slapped a lot, choked and pushed. Sean was saying things to hurt me and I was saying things to hurt him right back. We were riding to church one day and he tried to push me out of the car onto the Davison expressway. One time we tried to take a vacation from everything and went to Birch Run, Michigan to the outlet mall, and that was even a disaster. We tried to shop in order to clear our minds but all while we were there we only argued. On the way home Sean got fed up, pulled the car to the shoulder of the freeway, got out and started walking.

He just left me and our three kids sitting in the car on the shoulder of the freeway. I sat there for a while thinking he was going to come back. I didn't know where I was going but after a while I drove off and tried to find our way home. I eventually saw Sean walking and pulled up on him. "Are you going to get in?" I asked, and luckily he got in.

It was crazy to me because he was the one doing all of the bullshit but he was trying to make it seem like I was the one causing all of the problems. He'd tell me I was why we couldn't get any farther because I wouldn't trust him anymore. Maybe that was the truth because I didn't believe a damn thing he said to me from that point on. That's when I suggested that we get ourselves tested for any STD's because since he had pussy cum all over him it was obvious he was fucking Antoinette without a condom.

Sean went to see his doctor first and when he came home with his results I met him at the front door.

"What did they say," I asked as he stood there with his papers in his hand. He leaned against the door and shook his head while tears rolled down his face. "What did they say, what do you have?"

"The doctor said I have Chlamydia."

"What, you have Chlamydia again? This don't make no fucking sense! So you don't ever wear a condom when you cheat on me ha?"

The doctor gave Sean some medication and some health kits. Then I went to get some medicine from Dr. Hamrick because I had the shit too. One night we laid on the bed and had a serious conversation, and that time we were being honest.

"Do you remember after we got married, I asked were you cheating on me?"

"Yeah," he answered.

"Why did you lie to me then? Was it the same girl?"

"No, that time it was a girl name Darleen." I just sat there like *what the fuck?*

"Do you remember me giving you some pills and telling you I had strep throat? I just want you to see how much I be protecting you because you might think I didn't want this marriage. But I've been trying to make this marriage work because even after you gave me a STD, I still didn't want to argue, fuss or fight with you. I told you I had strep throat so you could take some medication. But the real reason I had the medication was because you gave me Chlamydia."

"Why didn't you tell me you knew?"

"For what, so we can argue, fuss or fight?" I was looking him in his face. "Sean I love you."

The things I did to get love. In my marriage I was the same as when I was teenager, looking for love in all the wrong places. I wanted him to love me so much but he didn't. I wanted it so bad but he didn't and it was like I almost became a slave for him because I knew he was doing me wrong and I didn't care. I just wanted to be wanted.

Everything he was doing to me was destroying me, and it all reflected on my childhood when I was told I was never going to be shit. I'm only going to be good for laying on my back. All I'm going to be is a housewife, if that. "Ain't no man ever gonna want you! You ain't gonna be nothing but a hoe!" That shit scarred me for life. And there I was in a marriage trying to prove a point, and it was sucking the life out me. It was killing me daily because I was so determined to what, make this man love me?

Chapter 10

Hooked

Me and Sean struggled and barely made it in our marriage. We fought like cats and dogs on a daily basis. The medication I was taking had taken over me and I wasn't myself anymore because I was popping pills right and left. I started having mental confusion and was straight up addicted to prescription drugs and didn't even know it.

There were more pills prescribed to me other than the ones I already mentioned. I was now taking Ativan, Vicodin and several other different pills Dr. Hamrick gave me that I couldn't pronounce. The medications were really affecting my mind and my way of thinking. I was sleeping a whole lot more than I normally did. I wasn't just dozing off during the day; I was sleeping for two, three and four days at a time. I would go to sleep on a Monday and wouldn't get up until Thursday. Then next time I'd wake up it would be Tuesday.

From my doctor telling me to double up on my medication I stayed drowsy and started having memory loss. I couldn't even remember the last time I had taken my medication and would constantly keep taking it. It got to the point where I was taking 160 pills in one day. It may sound unbelievable but it was happening. I couldn't remember taking them and I was only focused on "I know I have to take my medication." Nobody knew it but I was a straight up mentally ill patient and I needed some help.

That month of June my family came to Detroit for the church convention and they stayed at our house. I was so sick at the time that my brother Derrick would stay home with me and Faith while everybody else went to church day and night. Derrick told me sometimes I would stand up then fall straight to the floor because I couldn't walk. I would try to get up and cook but he'd stop me and do it himself. He told me about a lot of things I did and don't even remember.

My entire body was bruised up from fighting. While my family was in Detroit they asked me was Sean giving me the bruises? I told them no but the truth was I couldn't even remember where the bruises came from. I was always asleep so only Sean knew how I got bruised up.

I'd get up at three and four in the morning and go to Super Kmart. I'd drive myself there and not even remember because I was so drugged. Then I'd wake up a day or two later and thank Sean for going shopping for me.

"Bianca I didn't go to the store, you went to the store by yourself," was what he told me. I never remembered putting the key into the ignition or anything. I was blessed because God was keeping me in unseen danger. I know for a fact God had to been driving my car for me and taking me back and forth.

After that Sean started hiding the car keys from me so I wouldn't go anywhere. Then he started hiding my pills and when he did that, we started fighting a whole lot more. He was hiding my pills while I was an addict and you can't do that. So whenever he took my drugs I pitched a fit. "Where's my medicine? I need my medicine!" My body started having a breakdown and I needed my drugs. I was told by a doctor that my body was having a worse breakdown as opposed to someone who was on street drugs.

The controlled substances send signals to my brain and tell my brain to do whatever the pill was made to do. Just take my sleeping for an example. Even if I had been sleeping for five days straight, if I took another pill and when my brain got the signal, I was going back to sleep no matter what. Come to find out, I wasn't even sleeping. I was unconscious in a coma right in the privacy of my own home.

You may wonder, *well where was Sean? What was he doing? Didn't he know if you were asleep for that long then you needed some medical attention?* But the truth is I don't think he was fully aware of my situation just as I wasn't fully aware. Maybe he thought I needed to stay in the house and not try to drive myself around? Whatever it was, we weren't fully aware of how messed up I was. But my babies were aware. They would try to come into my bedroom and care for me.

I remember a time when I was in the bed and L'Tisha brought me a glass of foggy water and tried to make me drink it. "Mama wake up. You been sleep for a long time. You didn't eat for a long time. You didn't drink your water for a long time." She was trying to pour the water in my mouth while telling me this.

One time L'Tisha and Little Keith came into my room after they had made some toast for me. "Is she dead? Is she dead?" they asked each other. Little Keith was breaking the toast and trying to put it my mouth so I could eat it. Seeing my kids trying to care for me made me try to get up and get off the drugs. After the medication wore off and I woke up, Sean was nowhere to be found. Little Keith was basically caring for me and my other two kids all by himself.

That's when I took a good look at my kids and how much they had changed. The last I could remember my youngest child Faith, I had to carry her around in my arms, but then she was walking around. I don't have any memories of my little baby. I broke down and started crying when I realized I had been out of it for so long.

I guess Sean must have thought I was going to stay in my condition. When he came home and I explained to him what the medication was doing to me it was like he didn't believe me. When we'd get into it he called me a drug addict and that wasn't helping the situation at all. He called me a junkie and all kinds of names. He'd still hide my pills and we'd still fight because of it.

"Is this what you want?" he'd yell at me. "You want this? Is this what's gonna make you calm down?" Then he'd pour all the pills in his hand, open my mouth and try to shove the pills down my throat. I would try to fight him off of me as he would hold me down and try to pour a glass of water down my throat. He was supposed to been, but wasn't handling the situation the way it was supposed to be handled. He was only making things worse.

When Sean would get rid of my pills I would go back to Dr. Hamrick and he would gladly give me some new prescriptions. If I couldn't wait until the prescriptions were filled then he would give me some medication from his office to take with me. I had told him I wanted to come off of the medication, so he was giving me some morphine and Benadryl to help ease me off. And with me trying to come off of the medication my body was going through a lot of changes.

"Doctor Hamrick, I got the shakes," I explained, "and I'm cold and breaking into sweats."

"Okay, I'm going to give you this shot and it will help you feel better," he assured me. "Did you drive yourself?" When I answered yes he told me, "Well you're going to have to stay here and sleep it off for a while."

I did what he told me and the shot he gave me knocked me right out. When I woke up I was in the examining room all by myself, completely naked. I was drowsy as hell and couldn't believe I was sitting there naked. I looked around the room for my clothes and saw them on the floor. That's when Dr. Hamrick walked into the room. "Oh you're waking up," he said, then quickly gave me another shot. When I woke up again I was fully dressed.

I knew I had been raped by my doctor, but I was so strung out on the medication he was giving me that I didn't even care. I went back to Dr. Hamrick every time I needed some more drugs. I couldn't stop seeing him because I was hooked on drugs.

Chapter 11

136

There was a time when Sean and I had a fight over God knew what. I was so high off the medication at that time that I can barely remember what happened myself. But Sean, he remembers.

We were fighting each other when Sean had me on the floor slapping my face back and forth as hard as he could with is right hand. During the fight I went unconscious and when I woke up the paramedics were standing over me.

"Are you okay?" the paramedics asked with the strangest looks on their faces. "We need to take you to the hospital so please, if you can walk, please come with us."

"Okay, let me say good bye to my kids first."

"Noooooo!" they shouted as I started to walk to my kids bedrooms. Then before I knew it I blacked out again.

When I woke up, I was in Detroit Receiving Hospital's emergency room with my arms and feet tied to the bed. I looked over at my arms then I started screaming and hollering. The emergency staff was already standing over me when I woke up in shock. They all tried to calm me down the best way they could and that was by giving me some more medication. But the more I looked at my arms, the more I lost it.

"What happened to me? What happened to me?" I screamed over and over. That's when I was told I cut myself 136 times.

My arms, my stomach, neck, right wrist and back were all cut up. I didn't know what happened but I was told I cut myself.

"Bianca, do you know what happened?" they asked.

"No!!!" I screamed.

"We brought you in here because you cut yourself. Do you know you cut yourself?"

"No!!!"

When I looked at my arms and saw them all stitched up, the first thing I thought was somebody got me and tried to rape me or something. Or maybe I was in a horrible accident? I didn't know what happened. I still don't know what happened. I can only go by what was said to me.

The police report stated that Sean said we got into a verbal dispute then he went outside and sat in the car to cool off. When he came back into the house I was standing there all cut up... that's what he said... the domestic violence unit disagreed with that.

One reason why they disagreed was because when they came to the hospital to see me a female officer told me to never again say I cut myself.

"Ms Bianca, I want you to stop saying you did this to yourself."

"But they told me I did it to myself," I sobbed.

"Hold up your hand." She threw a bean bag at me and said, "Catch," so I caught it. "Now look at your wrist. Which wrist is cut?"

"My right wrist," I answered

"That's right, you are right handed. If you would've tried to kill yourself you would've slit your left wrist, not the right one." There was a brief pause then she said, "I'm going to give you an example of what I think happened. Yes, I believe you and your husband got into a verbal dispute. And I believe somewhere in the argument he lost it. He knew you were drugged, talking out of your head, and could barely function, then something you said made him snap. After he cut you on your back and throat he just went crazy and cut your arms. Then he had to cover it to make it look like you did it. So he slit your wrist."

She went on to tell me after Sean slit my wrist he realized I was passed out so he had to call 911. He couldn't get rid of my body so he had to come up with a story about what happened. She said she believed he slit my wrist because he panicked.

"The dumb bastard should've slit the left wrist," she said. "He tried to make it seem like you committed suicide to cover up what he did."

Sean gave the police an eyebrow arching blade and that was the weapon either me or him used to cut me up with.

The hospital staff stitched me up while I was unconscious, then they told me what happened when I woke up. Right after they let me talk to the police was when they sent me up to the mental floor. Then after a couple of hours they sent me home, same day in, same day out.

When I got home the Young People's Meeting was going on at church. Sean told me Bishop Duren wanted me to come see him as soon as I got out of the hospital, so I went to see him as soon as I got home. I sat in his office all bandaged up in white bandages. The blood was seeping through some of the bandages, but I didn't even care. All

Bishop Duren could do was look at me and ask what happened.

"I don't know." I answered him in a low voice with tears pouring down my face. "I don't know what happened."

"What happened?" he asked again.

"I don't know?"

"Who did this to you?"

"Me."

"No, No," he shook his head, "who did this to you?"

"Me." He asked me who did it to me over and over and my answer was, "I did it. They said I did it. Bishop, I don't know? I was passed out. I was pronounced dead on arrival." They took me to the hospital on a "code red" because I had lost so much blood.

Bishop Duren gave me some spiritual advice. He told me don't let the Devil fool me and he and the Lord loved me. He also told me we'll get through this… not I'll get through this, but we'll get through this. Before I walked out of his office he stood up to hug me and with my bandaged arms I hugged him back.

"You know I love you," he told me as we hugged.

"Yes Bishop I know."

"I love you." He leaned in closer to my face. "I love you," he told me with his face close to my face. "I love you," he said over and over and then he tried to kiss me on my lips.

I pulled back and tried to push away from him because I was confused. I really didn't know what he was trying to do, but even as I pulled back he kept hugging me and moving his face closer to my face. I really started to get nervous because he wouldn't let me go and was forcefully trying to kiss me on my lips.

"I love you," he told me one last time just before he finally let me go.

I was a little uncomfortable with the situation Bishop Duren and I were in because I didn't quite understand it. But Bishop Duren helped me out a whole lot as far as my cuts were concerned. He never turned down any of my phone calls no matter how late I called him.

"No matter what time of day or night, I'm here for you," he told me. And he was there. I don't think he knows it but he is the only person at that church who knew what was going on with me. Even the incident with Elder Cooley touching my breast, Bishop Duren was the only person I told it to since it happened. I also told him about Elder Thomas molesting me and Vic Mackeyva, even though he still allows them in his church. He told me Elder Thomas molested me because it happened to him. But even still, Bishop Duren has a special place in my heart because he was always there when I needed him.

There were times when I hated myself for doing some of the things I've done. And there were times when I didn't give a damn. When I left out of Bishop Duren's office I didn't give a damn and still stayed at the church for the Young People's Meeting. I walked amongst the people like nothing was wrong with me. I wasn't embarrassed or scared at the time and didn't care about what anybody had to say or ask me.

My Aunt Roslyn from Ohio was at the meeting and she was walking around the church looking for me. Sean had told her I was in the dressing room so she came in to see what happened to me. When I unwrapped the bandages and showed her what happened, her whole face instantly dropped. Tears rolled down her face as she turned her head and said, "Bianca, I can't look." But still for some reason I didn't care what people thought. I still went and sat in the service.

I handled the situation the best way I could. But Sean couldn't accept it when I told him the medication made me how I was. He really didn't want to believe it. He wanted to think I just all of a sudden started overdosing on pills and that completely destroyed our already messed up marriage.

As time passed Sean wanted us to get out more and start going to church picnics. But I was feeling like this small and so unattractive therefore I didn't want to go. All I wanted to do was isolate myself. Then not even 30 days after I got cut up we had a fight. We fought because I was in a rage and wanted some answers about what happened.

"What happened?" I shouted at him. He was there and knew what happened, so I wanted some answers! "If I was the only person around you and you woke up all cut the fuck up you're going to want to know what happened!"

All Sean said was we were arguing.

"What do you mean we were arguing? What were we arguing about?"

"You started talking about Antoinette Davenport," he told me.

"We've had arguments about her a million times before! It never led to nothing like this! What the fuck do you mean?"

I questioned him over and over to the point where I got mad as hell and started fighting him. I wouldn't even say I was mad as hell! I'd say I was hell itself! I didn't know if he did this to me! I was laying in the bed at night with a man and didn't even know if he did this to me! So yes, we fought like hell and he didn't make it any better.

"You're crazy," he constantly told me. "You are insane!"

That really hurt me at the time because I didn't care what nobody said. **I KNEW I WASN'T CRAZY OR INSANE!**

Sometimes I told myself I was past it and it didn't affect me. I tried to act like I didn't notice the cuts. I didn't look at them. I tried to forget all about it because I didn't feel like facing it. The whole situation was a mystery to me and I didn't like talking about it with anybody.

There were other situations I got past, like the child molestation and domestic violence I was raised in. But this one, I'm still not over it. I even lie to myself when I say I'm over the molestation. I'm dealing with the cuts and the biggest issue I face with them is not knowing what happened? I don't have a clue. I'm totally blank. No matter how hard I try to remember back to when it happened, I can only remember what was told to me. So it's like I have to take everybody else's word because I was drugged.

I got a reaction from people whenever they saw my cuts for the first time. After it happened I stopped going out of the house. I missed an entire church convention, and that was rare for me. When people saw me it was in the winter season when I was completely covered up, but when summer came back around it started to haunt me all over again.

When it first happened I disappeared and started popping even more pills. I didn't want to be awake to face my situation. I didn't want to see myself. When I took showers and baths I took them with the lights off. When I came out to go shopping I wore sheer blouses with the sleeves coming all the way down to the middle of my palm. Then I would wear a big watch so the slit on my wrist wouldn't show.

Sean was ashamed of the situation because people would take one look at me and say, "Oh she's crazy. She's mentally insane."

After a while I started seeking help from other doctors concerning my condition but every doctor I saw told me, "You have to take your medicine. When was the last time you took your medicine?" I was trying to stop taking the medication. Sometimes I would get mad and flush the medication down the toilet, then find myself back in Dr. Hamrick's office getting some more medication the next day.

When I say help was not available I really mean it was not available, especially in my case because people were judging me by my cuts. When I went to see different doctors and psychologists, off the top, they would think I was suicidal. They thought I was crazy and insane. First of all, I was depressed as hell when I walked into their offices. I couldn't even say two words without tears rolling down my face. I felt totally hopeless but I was seeking help from anybody I could and they all asked me the same question.

"When did you last take you medication?"

"I stopped taking the medication."

"No, you can't stop. Did your doctor take you off?"

They were talking to me from what they learned in medical school and they weren't really trying to listen to what I had to say. Nobody was listening to me and that was so fucked up because everybody was judging me from my outer appearance. They were looking at me as if I was suicidal and everybody was telling me what I didn't want to hear.

"Take your medication. You shouldn't have stopped taking your medication. You have to wait until your doctor weans you off of the medication."

I thought to myself, *they must be crazy if they think I'm going to keep taking something they said made me do this to myself. To cut myself 136 times? Or to even allow somebody else to cut me 136 times? Never feeling it and not even remembering it? Is that crazy or is that crazy? Why would I keep taking that? I would be crazy as hell to keep shoving it down my throat.*

Since everybody I went to was telling me the same shit, I ended up going back Dr. Hamrick. He was the only one who could stop the compulsive reactions my body was having, like the chills and the shakes. He was the only one who was helping my drug cravings. He helped the pain and aching by prescribing me different medication and giving me the shots he was giving me in his office. He was the only one who had a cure after all my medicine was gone.

At first I was going through a thirty-day supply of medication in three weeks. Then it went to two weeks. Two weeks turned into one week. Next thing I knew I was taking 160 pills in one day, again. In one fucking day I was taking that many pills. But what was I to do? I went to everybody I knew who were licensed. I went to Bishop Duren. My husband didn't believe me. People in the church thought I was crazy. My doctor was taking his own medicine. So what was I to do?

When I got cut up I couldn't feel a thing, that's how medicated and out of it I was. Getting cut up had to be painful because the cuts were so deep that right now they look like keloids all over my body. The cut on my wrist was so deep that I don't have any feeling in it anymore because I was told I cut into the nerve. The doctors at the hospital said the amount of medication I had in my body when I got cut up was enough medication to perform a major surgery. I had actually taken that much medication and was walking around arguing and fighting with my husband. If anything would've happened to me I wouldn't have felt it.

I have 136 cuts on my body... all over my body. The cut on my legs have healed and vanished but the rest of my body is scarred for life.

And even right now everybody still asks me, "What happened?" If I go to a hospital right now they'll ask, "What happened? Who did this to you?" It's like the big mystery, "Who did this to you?" I don't know who did it... even after all the bullshit Sean put me through I can't say, *Sean did it! He did it!* I can't say it because I don't know if he did it. So I say I did it, but I don't know if that's true either. So what was I to do?

Chapter 12

Mentally Insane

Because I desperately wanted some help I ended up checking myself into a mental institution. I went to Sinai Grace Hospital because I was out of my mind and losing it. The cuts were having a really big mental effect on me. Plus, by me trying to stop taking the medication at the same time, it was too much for me. My body was going through all kinds of different things and I had a nervous breakdown.

The hospital thought it would be best if they admitted me into a mental institution because I was so stressed out and depressed about the cuts. I had to agree to being admitted because I wasn't suicidal. Therefore I agreed and signed the papers that admitted me into Oakwood Heritage Mental Facility.

At the institution I was interviewed, examined, and then asked, "Honey what's wrong?" They didn't think anything was wrong with me until they saw my cuts. When they saw the cuts they were like, "Oh my God!" I was put into a room with about twenty five people who were really insane but they had me there for being suicidal.

The patients there were really gone and there was no help for their conditions. Most if not all of them were not snapping back to reality ever again. Because I was the sane patient around a bunch of insane people everybody thought I worked there. They thought I was a new doctor. The staff walked around and asked, "Who's the new lady?" When they found out I was a sane patient they moved me from the rest of the patients and put me with some patients who were more in their right frames of mind.

My roommate's name was Carrie and she was schizophrenic, but when I first saw her she appeared to be normal. I realized she had a problem when she introduced me to her best friend who wasn't there. As I stood looking out of our room window she came over to me and told me my hair was pretty.

"Your hair is so pretty. It's so long. Is it your real hair? Can I play in your hair?"

"I don't care," I told her as I stared out of the window at the real world.

The windows were made for people like me who was in the state of mind that I was in. I looked at the thick bullet proof looking glass thinking, *they had to know what was going through people's heads when they put these windows in here because it's going through my head right now. If these were regular windows I'd run straight through it.* That's how angry I was. I was mad about what happened to me and I felt trapped by it. Every day I was there made me want to give up because every day the facility made me feel like the situation was getting worse. I thought, *oh my God I can't believe I'm in this situation. I'm in a fucking mental hospital!*

I had ten days to be there and prove to them I was better in order to leave. Or, if the staff felt like I needed to stay they would take me before a Judge in a courtroom that was downstairs and he would make the decision. I basically signed over my rights when I signed in. They could've made me an award of the State if they felt like I couldn't go home and function properly.

Sometime later after Carrie had been all in my face trying to be my friend, we had to go to the staff desk for our night time medication. Carrie didn't realize I was standing right behind her as she talked to the staff about me.

"I don't want to go to bed," Carrie complained to the staff.

"What's wrong Carrie," the staff asked. "Why don't you want to go to bed?"

"Because... well, I want to go to bed but I want to change my room."

"Why do you want to change your room?"

"Because of my roommate."

"Are you talking about Bianca?" the staff member looked at me like *don't say nothing.*

"I'm scared of my roommate."

"You're scared of Bianca? Bianca is a sweetheart. Why are you scared of her?"

"Come here," Carrie used her finger and whispered. "Because she know too much."

"Because what?" the staff member asked making sure I heard what she said.

"Because she know too much. That girl know more then everybody in here!"

What Carrie said did something to me. The insane people even knew I had no business being in a place like that. She made me want to shake myself off and tell myself, *you don't have to keep telling yourself you are not crazy! Even the crazy people who's been in here for years can see that you are not crazy! They're going up to the staff saying,*

"Get her out of here! She's not like us! She knows too much!"

My doctor in the institution was a short Chinese man and every time he spoke to me he never looked me in my eyes. Then after three days my doctor popped off and told me I was bipolar.

"I feel that you are bipolar and you should take this medication," he told me without looking at me.

"What's making you feel like that? First of all you're telling me you think I'm bipolar, not that I am bipolar."

"You are showing signs of being bipolar. So I have the proof that you are bipolar." He started writing out all kinds of prescriptions and started telling me he wanted me to take this kind of medication and that kind of medication.

"You want me to go by your feelings and let you shove some pills down my throat?" As he kept writing the prescription I told him, "No."

"What do you mean no? This is better for your health."

"First of all, you've talked to me for three days and you haven't looked me in my face. You don't know if I'm black, white or Chinese. All you know is what you have on a piece of paper. How can you tell me I'm bipolar and you never even took a look at me or examined me? You haven't run any tests on me and you want me accept what you feel?

Because you haven't even looked at me, I personally feel like you are not a professional doctor."

For the first time he looked up at me. I guess he was used to people who couldn't speak up for themselves because they were sick. But that wasn't my case. I wanted someone to help my situation, not to continue to shove pills down my throat.

"I believe this medication will help you," he told me.

"I feel the medication will only make me worse," I told him in response. "The medication is the problem. I have chronic asthma and upper respiratory disease. I have a doctor who put me on all these crazy medications and told me it will help me feel better and relax."

"Well, I think you need it."

"I know I don't need it. I have too much medication in me and I want to come off."

"Oh that can't happen because you're on too many medications. We can't just take you off like that or you would be sick and mentally confused."

"That's why I'm here. If you look in your book it'll tell you. I stopped taking my medication and I flushed them down the toilet."

"Well, you have to take these five medications."

"No."

"Well take these four."

"No."

"Take these three."

"No."

"What about two."

"No."

"One."

"No. What about none?"

"If you are going to be here then we have to have you on some kind of medication." That was basically to show that they were trying to make some type of effort to help me. "How about a half of pill?" he asked.

I agreed so he put me on half of a depression pill. I took the half of a pill because I figured it wouldn't hurt me. And by my tolerance level for medication being so high the half of a pill did absolutely nothing for me.

By my fourth day in the institution I was ready to go home. The patients were fighting each other and the facility wasn't being run correctly. They had a couple of staff members on every floor and on every floor there were twenty male and female patients. The women were on one side of the floor, the men were on the other side and the staff desk sat in the middle. All of us watched TV and ate our meals in the same room and there were so many crazy things happening during those times.

I ended up speaking with a social worker who the State had sent in to check up on things. She went around the room and asked everybody to tell her something about the facility. She wanted to know about how we were being treated and how was the facility was being run? When it was my turn to talk I told her about the situation with the Chinese doctor and as I told her everybody started to applaud. As everybody was clapping for me she looked at me and took her glasses off.

"Bianca, I'd like to see you after group," she told me. After group she told me, "I want you to know you stand out from everybody else. If nobody else can see it I want you to know I see it. God bless you for standing up for yourself.

She read through my files to see what was going on with me and she believed me as far as what I said about the doctor. She said I was an inspiration to her from the way I was able to stand up for myself while being in an institution and telling them I was improperly medicated.

While living in the mental facility, whenever somebody saw my cuts they said, "Oh my God! Oh Lord! Who did this to you?" I got so sick of seeing and hearing people's response when they saw me that it was tearing me apart. It was so depressing while I was there.

At the mental institution I decided that I wanted out of my marriage. That was because I had time to sit back and examine my life up until that point. I asked myself, "How did I get here? How in the hell did I get here? Out of all the places in the world, Bianca, you are here! What the hell?"

When I thought about me being there it all reflected on my husband. When I went to one-on-one counseling we reflected on my husband.

"I understand what you are trying to do by coming off the medication," the counselor explained to me. "But the first thing you need to do is get rid of that man who is causing you the stress and acute asthma attacks." I found out some of my asthma attacks were actually panic attacks that were caused by him cheating on me and fighting me.

I listened to a lot of the advice the counselor gave me. After that I took some more time to think. Then I came to the conclusion that I was going to tell Sean I didn't want the marriage anymore. Even Bishop Duren told us to our faces he didn't believe I cut myself up all by myself. We said I did it but he said he didn't believe it, and if I did do it Bishop Duren said Sean drove me to do it. He also said Sean drove me to the medication because of the things he was putting me through.

What Bishop Duren told us replayed through my mind over and over about how "HE" was the cause. I remember when even Dr. Hamrick told me he was the cause of my asthma. That's when I went to the phone, called Sean, then told him I wanted him to pack his bags and leave. I didn't care where he went but when I got home he couldn't be there. And if he didn't leave then I was going to leave.

I'd had enough. At that point, I was looking at my body and my state of mind and realized I was the person who back in high school used to be so beautiful and could sing in front of hundreds of people. "I'm not supposed to be here!"

"No Bianca, you don't want this," Sean pleaded on the phone. "I'm going to do better. I know it's hard for you. I know it's the medication. I'm sorry Bianca." The sad part about it was I talked to my kids and found out Sean was cheating on me while I was in the mental hospital.

After ten days I was discharged from the mental hospital.

"We hate to see you go but we're happy you're leaving," the staff told me. They had gotten attached to me from the conversations we had.

"I have a strong feeling I'm going to see you again," one woman told me who I had told all about Dr. Hamrick. "I don't know where I'm going to see you, but I know I'm going to see you. With that will power and determination you have, I might see you on TV telling your story."

Chapter 13

The Worst Thing I Ever Did

When I got home Sean had a bag packed the way that I asked him to have it. Soon as I walked into the house I asked him, "Where's your bag?" He was being extra nice to me to the point where it was obvious he was doing it on purpose. He knew it was about to be over and he didn't want to mess it up. But I wasn't telling him I wanted a divorce. I was telling him, "Right now we need to separate. You need to go your way and I need to go my way. If it's meant for us to be together then the Lord will give us back to each other."

But still he didn't leave! And by me being so damn nice, loving, forgiving and caring, my dumb stupid ass allowed him to stay. And to make matters worse I stayed myself. I probably stayed because I didn't have anywhere else to go. Where was I going to go with three kids? But nothing changed and the arguing and fighting continued so that's when I went to a shelter.

I ended up going to a shelter at least four times because I didn't have any family I could go to. I didn't want to put our business in the church anymore so I didn't have any church people to go to. I didn't have anybody so it was just me and kids, fighting, trying to fend for our lives. At that point life was feeling like somebody was choking me to the point of where I couldn't breathe. And the same person who was choking me was the same person who I was having sympathy for and allowing to him stay with me. I was steadily trying to make the marriage work but knowing within myself it was dead. And what is dead needs to be buried.

Around that time Bishop Duren made Sean a Deacon at the church so he should've had some type control over himself. He was getting up preaching about this and that to the Young Peoples Department at church and he couldn't even control himself. But he wanted to talk to somebody else. I used to sleep on the couch a lot and he'd always come in there with me.

"Bianca, you can get back in the bed. I'm sorry. I was wrong. Just be patient with me because I'm going through a lot right now."

Sean took my kindness for weakness and the more I forgave him the worse he treated me. I guess he felt like I needed him plus he even told me with his own mouth.

"You need me because you ain't shit! You ain't never gonna be shit, ain't that what Elder Cooley said? He was right! You ain't never gonna be nothing! You're crazy and your childhood got you all fucked up in the head! I'm not the one who molested you! I'm not the one who beat your mama! I'm not the one who abused you!"

"No, you're not the one," I told him, "you're someone who's worse!"

Right after that I tried to kill Sean by poisoning his food. I took some green rat poison and put it in his green beans after I had cooked diner. I took the little peas out of the green beans and pushed the rat poison in with a toothpick so he wouldn't see it. I was tired and I had a numb feeling over me. When he sat down at the table I sat in front of him and watched him say his grace.

"How much do you love me?" I asked him.

"Bianca, baby you know I love you. But you be trippin' sometimes."

"Oh yeah, you love me? Well how much do you think I love you?"

"Well... I know a part of you hates me for what I've done but..." Soon as he said "But" I cut him off.

"Do you ever fear that I might one day pay somebody to have you knocked off?" He was getting ready to put his green beans into his mouth. "Or do you think I might poison your food?"

"You wouldn't do that."

"I wouldn't? Check your green beans. Cut them open and look." When he cut the green beans open he saw the rat poison. "You better be careful what you do to me."

Sean got up and pushed his plate to the floor. Later on that evening he changed his attitude.

"You know what, if I was in your shoes I would've left a long time ago," he told me. "I understand why you're mad."

Even though he said he understood we still got into it the next night. He was mad and getting ready to walk out of the door when I started yelling at him.

"Go ahead and leave! Go to those hoes! Run to them like you always do! Its fine, but I hope you come back and stay here with the kids because I'm leaving too! I got somebody coming to pick me up!" He was at the door getting ready to walk out then he stopped and came back.

"Oh you cheatin' on me? You cheatin' on me?"

"Yeah I'm cheating on you too! How do it feel when the shoe is on the other foot?"

"You cheatin' on me?" He hit a glass picture frame that was hanging on the wall over my head. "Answer me!" then he started hitting the wall.

I got on the phone and acted like I was calling somebody, but I called the Jacksonville, Florida number for the time. But Sean thought I was calling a man and I wanted him to get a taste of his own medicine.

"Okay, you'll be here," I faked on the phone. "Well he's getting ready to walk out the door right now."

Sean hit another picture on the wall and cut his hand. Then he took his bloody hand that still had glass in it and he smeared his blood all over my face. Then he walked through the house and broke every piece of glass he saw with his bare hand. He was pissed the fuck off but I was satisfied because he got a taste of his own medicine.

I tried to be strong but I just couldn't do it. Because of all the fighting we were doing I started drinking. Then I started smoking cigarettes which was something I had never done. I was all fucked up in the head at that point. When Sean would come in the house I would leave out the door and walk the streets. I had started to give up. Then I did the worse thing I could've ever done. I went back to Dr. Hamrick for some more drugs.

At that point I was taking narcotics with straight shots of gin and vodka. I was becoming what they wanted me to become, a fucking junkie! "I'm crazy! If y'all say I'm crazy, then oh well, I'm crazy!" I gave in because it was me against the world and if you can't beat 'em then join 'em. And that's just what I did, I joined in on everything. If you wanted to fight then we was about to fight. You want to cheat on me, well I can cheat too. You want to lie to me, then I'm about to start lying too. You want to make me feel like shit, then I going to make you feel like shit too!

So now it was about even. That was the point I was at. I didn't give a fuck about his feelings so our fights got worse. Sean had another phone line installed in our house so he could talk to some woman he was fooling around with. When I found out he was talking to another woman on the new phone line we got into it. He pushed me against the wall so I threw a box of cereal at him. When the cereal hit him, he then grabbed me by my neck and started to strangle me. I started punching him and as we were fighting L'Tisha started running up the stairs screaming and hollering.

We fought from the kitchen to down the hallway. Our daughter Faith was walking around in the way of us. He punched me in my face and the punched knocked me from the hallway to the dining room and I landed on top of Faith. Then he got on top of me, grabbed me by the back of my head and started banging my head into the floor.

When Little Keith heard the commotion he ran down the hallway to see what was going on. I'll never forget being down on the floor being punched and beat by a man and looking into my son's eyes at the same time. Little Keith had one foot in front of him and the other behind him with his eyes wide open not knowing what to do. He didn't know if he should help or not because it was the person who was his daddy and he was supposed to respect him. But at the same time he was on top of his mother hurting her. Little Keith was trapped in the middle and I could see the war going on in his eyes. So on that day I promised myself I wouldn't let my kids be raised up the same way I was.

We struggled on the floor until I was able to get him off of me. I got up and pushed him into the hallway and he slammed me into the wall. Then he pushed me into Faith's room and slammed me into her wooden baby crib shattering it to pieces. Right after that the fight stopped and I called the police while telling Sean, "This is it, I want you out!"

When the police came Sean was gone like always because he was guilty.

"When he comes back, call us again and we'll come get him," the police told me. They saw the bruises all over me. My head was once again busted open and my lip was bleeding all over the place. I had a boot print in my back that was from three days ago when I had drugged myself and didn't know what was going on. I had to ask my kids about what happened.

"Were your daddy and I fighting?"

"Yes Ma'am," they told me.

"What happened?"

"Daddy kicked you down the stairs."

When Sean finally came home he unhooked the house phone and hid it so I couldn't call the police. When he went to sleep I took the house and car keys off of his key ring. I knew he wouldn't notice them because he had a ton of keys on the ring. I let him walk out of the door that next morning plus I even kissed him on his cheek like everything was okay.

"See you this evening baby," was what I told him.

"Alright, goodbye baby," he told me back.

When he walked out of the house I locked the door behind him. A minute later he was trying to get back into the house by banging on the door.

"Bianca, let me in!"

We lived next door to some members of our church so he went to their house and told them what happened. When he came back I still wouldn't let him in so he walked away and stayed gone for three hours before he came back begging again.

"Bianca, would you please open the door? Please let me in!"

"No! Let you in for what?" He walked away and came back but that time I didn't even bother going to the door.

I figured he'd be back later on that night because it was October and he wouldn't walk around all night in the cold. So when night came I heard a loud banging on the door. The knock was so loud that it scared my kids so I took them upstairs. As I came back downstairs the banging started on the back door. I didn't even bother to look out the window and soon enough the banging stopped.

The next morning I got up bright and early then went Downtown to get a personal protection order against Sean. When I made it back home everything was cool but when night came Sean came back. He banged on the door but I didn't answer and he stopped. Ten minutes later the banging started again and that time it was extremely loud so I went to the window. I was going to tell him to stop banging on the door so hard or else I was going to call the police but when I looked out of the door the police were standing there along with him.

I opened the door for the officers with my restraining order in my hand. The same officers who had been to my house on other occasions and had saw me all cut up were the same officers who were standing there with him. These were the same officers who told me I didn't cut myself and to get a protection order and have Sean locked up.

"Officers, how are you?" I asked. "If you're going to escort him in then you have to escort me and my kids out!"

"What's the problem?" One officer asked. I explained how we had a fight and he beat me up in front of my kids and when I finished the officer said, "Ma'am, he said you have the keys to his car."

"It's not his car. You can run the plate. "The car is in my name," I explained.

Sean bought the car and gave it to me but now he was trying to take it back and say that it's his.

"Why did you tell us it was your car," they asked Sean. "This car is in her name. You lied to us." I had already given the officer the keys to the car like *go ahead he can take it and leave* but the officer gave the keys back to me.

"Here are the keys to your car."

"If he's coming in, then I'm leaving out." I held up my protection order, "If he come in I have to leave out."

"They can stay," Sean all of a sudden decided. Sean walked away and my kids and I stayed in the house.

So we were on our own and nobody saw or heard from us for a long time. I had no idea where Sean was but he was calling the house back to back. Maybe he was calling so much because for the first time he figured out I'd had enough. He was gone for two weeks and that was the longest we'd ever been separated. And maybe that was the reason why he was calling me all day wanting to come back home.

"No Sean, we need to stay separated," I explained. "I'm not going to live with you and let my kids see us fight. I'm not going to do that to my kids."

"It's going to be different Bianca, I promise."

"You said that last time."

Sean left the house in October and next thing I knew October turned into January and I hadn't seen him. At that point, I think I was beyond a drug addict. I was running through my thirty day supply of pills in two and three days. I was always sick and constantly throwing up because I couldn't keep any food on my stomach. I had lost thirty pounds and was looking like a crack-head. There was a rumor going around the church saying me and another Sister were snorting powder together.

Chapter 14

Vengeance Is The Lords

My son had started school at the Pentecostal Church of God Christian Academy. Therefore, I would go to the school and help out with the other parents. I tried to help out as much as I could but at the same time I was still a junkie. A Sister who was my friend noticed that I couldn't stay focused on one thought so she used to try and talk to me about my problems. "I know something is wrong with you Bianca. I don't know what it is but I know something is wrong. So if you need me I'm here for you."

I started calling the Sister almost every night while I was fucked up and depressed. Besides Bishop Duren, she was the only person who knew everything. My own mother didn't even know what was going on with me.

"Bianca, you need to tell somebody," the Sister told me. But I really didn't tell anybody. I was trying to handle everything by myself and it overwhelmed me.

Then to make my situation even more fucked up, my son got molested in the bathroom at church one Sunday.

Little Keith told me he had to go to the bathroom during service so I sent him by himself. Next thing I know I was being asked to go downstairs by the usher. Little Keith was in the basement accompanied by Evangelist Hart. Keith had ran to Evangelist Hart and told him how some boy in the bathroom had molested him. The boy had supposedly gone back up to the service so we had Little Keith go and point him out. Sure enough, the boy was in the service and when Keith pointed him out from the back of the church we seen he wasn't another little boy. The boy was nineteen years old and had been a member of the Pentecostal Church of God his whole life.

I was furious and wanted to talk to Bishop Duren right away so he could do something about it. Sean just so happened to be at church that Sunday and together we called Bishop Duren's house and told him we needed to see him. Bishop made an appointment with us for the next day and when the day came, we were there bright and early.

In Bishop Duren's office I told him everything that happened at church the day before. Then I told him I wanted to call the police on the boy who molested my son. I also told him about the physical things I wanted to do to the boy.

"No," Bishop Duren cut me off and said. "Vengeance is the Lords. I'll talk to the boy's father and we'll straighten out all of this."

We left out of Bishop Duren's office feeling assured that everything was going to be handled. Sean went his way and I went mine. That next morning I got an unexpected visit from Evangelist Hart. He went around to all of the parent's homes who had children in grade K at the Pentecostal Church of God Christian Academy. He let us know they had evidence that someone had been sexually fondling the kindergarteners at school. And when it came down to my son, it brought up all the memories of what had happened to me when I was a kid at the Pentecostal Church of God.

"Molestation is something big that's happening in our church right now," Evangelist Hart explained to me as I sat in my lounge chair. "God ain't pleased with all that stuff and we want to reveal all these people who are doing such things. So many of us has been molested and raped by people we feel we shouldn't tell on because they may have leadership or something behind their name. Maybe even Pastor or Minister behind their name."

I'll never forget what he said when he got ready to leave.

"Even if somebody has done it to you, you need to reveal it, you need to tell." I felt so hurt knowing somebody did and could've been molesting my baby at his school. It hurt me so much to where it brought back memories of my own childhood and how Elder Thomas used to molest me. I didn't reveal anything to Evangelist Hart. Instead, I just focused on what he told me. "If it happened to you, you need to reveal it."

Besides, I was assured that Bishop Duren was going to make sure justice be served like he said he would. But as time went on absolutely nothing happened. The situation was forgotten about like all of the other child molestations that happened at the Pentecostal Churches of God in Detroit, Florida and around the country.

And even though nothing was done about it, did I get up and do anything about it myself? No I didn't. The reason why I didn't, I don't know? What could I do? This was my church I was dealing with and Bishop Duren told me not to do anything. He told all of us not to do anything; all meaning the molestation victims who told him about what happened to us.

I told my molestation story to a Sister from Indiana. We all were in Detroit at a meeting when we talked in the bathroom.

"Bianca, I believe you," she told me in tears. "My daddy did the same thing to me and my sister for as long as I can remember. That's why he don't live with us anymore. Now he lives here in Detroit. Bishop Duren lets him preach in the pulpit even though I told him what happened. And now he's just had another daughter with a Sister from Detroit and she knows all about this too."

Our lives were being destroyed by that church but we were blinded by love and couldn't see it. We've been molested in our homes by church members, in the bathrooms at church by church members, in the balcony at the Detroit church, and in the church school. Every one of us who's been molested has had a wild life afterwards, but everybody blames us for the way we grew up. But it's not our fault, we were molested at church and nobody did anything about it!

♫ ♫ ♫ ♫ ♫

One night I put my kids to bed then around two o'clock in the morning Antoinette Davenport pulled into my driveway. Remind you, Sean had been gone since October and when I had went to some of my doctor appointments I passed by her street and saw his car in her driveway. So I already knew he was still messing around with her.

She pulled up in my driveway blowing the horn in her car and screaming Sean's name. I had just got off the phone with my friend from church and was startled when I heard the commotion. "What do you want," I opened the door and yelled. "What do you mean Sean? He's not here so get the fuck out of my driveway!"

She pulled out of the driveway and drove to the corner of the street. By that time I was putting on my shoes and coat and on my way out of the door. It was about two inches of fresh snow on the ground and when I made it to the sidewalk she turned around and sped past me. She hit the brake at the next corner and did a 360 in the middle of the street then sped off.

I went back in the house and called Sean.

"Look, your bitch is coming over here looking for you! This is the type of shit I'm talking about! Me and my kids shouldn't have to go through nothing like this!" From me screaming on the phone my kids had woken up scared.

"Mama is Daddy out there?" they asked me.

After I told Sean what I had to say, he told me he didn't know what I was talking about then hung up in my face. So I sat on the floor with my back against the wall. I was already messed up because I was a junkie, so the first thing I did when I was under pressure was ran and popped some pills. I took my pills with some gin and not long after that I was just as drugged as I was when I didn't remember driving to the store. Then next thing I knew was I went in my bedroom and went to sleep, but when I woke up I was in jail.

In jail the police told me I took a golf club over to Antoinette Davenport's house, bust out her window, went into her house through the window and stood over her bed crying. Antoinette said I was asking her, "Where's Sean? Where's Sean? I know he's here, where is he?"

I was taken to the Wayne County Jail and stayed there for about a week. When I came to my senses I called Bishop Duren so he could come and bond me out. He told me he would bond me out but if he couldn't make it himself he would send someone to get me.

While I was in jail they made me take a psychiatric evaluation and this was when I started to remember what was going on with me. I remember the correction officers coming to our unit to do a shack-down and they made all of us get naked. We took off all of our clothes and I stood in line as ten female officers all said at the same time, "Oh my God! Look at her! Officer Williams, look at her!" They all gathered around me and said, "Baby, put your cloths back on. Who did this to you?"

They turned why I was there into a totally different situation.

"Ms, we want to help you. Who cut you up like that? You don't have to be scared. We want to help you." But I was all fucked up in the head so I didn't say anything.

Later on an officer came and told me somebody was there to bond me out.

"Who is it?" I asked. "Is it a man named Bishop Duren?"

"It's a young man," she answered.

"Ma'am, if that man's name is Sean, he's my husband. I have a restraining order against him and he's not supposed to be near me. Y'all can lock me back up because I'm not going nowhere with him. Put me back in my cell and I'll wait three to six months for my court date before I go back home with him."

That situation reminded me of the same dysfunctional situation that happened when I was a kid. I had the police officers and my mother right there, but the house was so messed up that I chose the back of the police car. "Put me in back of the police car." I was in the same situation but years later in my own marriage. "Put me back in my cell." I reflected back on my childhood and thought, *what the hell? I can't get away from this domestic violence! I can't win for losing!*

They made me change out of my jail clothes then took me into the lobby of the jail and that's when I saw Sean and his father standing there.

"Is that him?" the officers asked me.

"Yeah, that's him!" I answered. So they took me back. I changed back into my jail clothes and went back to my cell. I would've rather stayed in jail where I knew there was going to be some decency and order then to go with Sean. I didn't have to be in jail trying to fight my own battles because there was going to some decency and order no matter what.

So I stayed in jail and Sean sent his father back to get me. His father was one of the same people who seen the cuts on my body and asked,

"Who did this to you? Did my son do this to you? I understand he's my son but if he did this to you then you need to let somebody know."

"No, Sean didn't do it... they said I did it." I told him like I told everybody else.

Sean's father bonded me out and took me home. On the way there he told me,

"You know you were wrong for what you did."

"Yeah, but if it wasn't for your son bringing this woman into our life this would've never happened."

"Well you're right," he agreed.

170

When I made it home Sean sent the kids over by one of his sisters. After that I was going back and forth to court for the case I caught. The Court had me mentally evaluated and after the evaluation the psychiatrist said, "This woman is most definitely temporarily insane." I was temporarily insane was how they put it. So after months of going to court, the Judge sentenced me to five years of probation and outpatient treatment for my temporary insanity.

Not long after my sentencing I had to go to the FIA office to take care of some business. Then God forbid, I had to see Antoinette Davenport while I was there.

"This bitch had to be here," I said to myself.

"I ain't no bitch!" she yelled back.

"You is a bitch! You a motherfucking hoe too! Fuck you, I'll get your supervisor because I wasn't even talking to you!"

I talked to the supervisor and let her know what was going on and then I ended up leaving. Not long after that the bitch put a restraining order out against me claiming I came up to her job and harassed her. The bitch even had the nerve to get me and my kids' Medicaid and food stamps cut off. The company came to my house and took my oxygen tank away from me because it wasn't being paid for. So I went to Bishop Duren about it and told him I wanted to sue the lady.

"No, let the Lord handle it," Bishop Duren told me. "Don't worry about it, vengeance is the Lord's." So I did what he said while my kids and I were being treated like shit.

Then to make matters even more messed up, Antoinette Davenport claimed my kids were being neglected and sent some social workers to my house to take my kids away from me. When that happened I panicked and called my mother. I told my mother to come get my kids because the State was trying to take them away from me. When I called her it was on a Sunday and she was at my house that Monday night. She hopped in the car with Elder Cooley and drove to Michigan nonstop because she's crazy about her grandchildren.

The social worker came before my mother arrived and when she looked around my house she told me, "We apologize, we see no signs of neglect." Even though I was drugged I was still taking care of my kids. When my mother got there the first thing she said was I had lost too much weight. I was skinny as hell because I was a junkie but she really didn't know about it.

It was a little after ten p.m. and my mother and Elder Cooley were sitting in my living room. My phone just so happen to ring and it was one of the few Sisters from the church who I was cool with.

"Turn on Fox Two News," she told me. When I turned the news on the Fox 2 Problem Solvers were doing an investigation on Dr. Hamrick.

"Ain't that your doctor?" my mother asked. Right then everybody looked at me differently.

"Man Bianca, we didn't know."

This is how I know there is a God because when nobody would believe me, even when I was telling the doctors my medicine was making me sick, there was one man who fought back. This man's wife popped up dead and she was a patient of Dr. Hamrick. He went to the Fox 2 News Problem Solvers and said, "Hey wait a minute, this place needs to be checked out! I took my wife to this doctor and now she's dead!"

And I know exactly why he took her there. He took her there because she was going through what I was going through. Dr. Hamrick pumped her with morphine and Demerol then he probably raped her. The man got his wife home and she collapsed and died on the floor. Cause of death, overdose of morphine.

After that I started getting all kinds of help from people. The Medicaid company was finally talking to me when just before they wouldn't. People were on the phone with me who I didn't even know, telling me when they read my book they can say "I know that lady! I remember that

173

lady and the state of mind she was in. It was me who told her 'Don't give up!' " Strangers on the phone who worked for companies that I called were encouraging me all because my doctor was exposed. I felt so good after that.

It's amazing how something has to be exposed on TV or somebody has to die before someone is helped. Because of a lady dying, I got a chance to get my life back because Dr. Hamrick was being exposed. There's a part of me that wish I knew the man whose wife died. Because of him fighting back I got my life back.

It was reported that Dr. Hamrick had lost his license in another state for drugging and raping his patients. Later he was found guilty of illegal distribution of controlled substances and was sentenced to four years in a federal prison.

I went to church and testified about everything and when I say everything I mean I exposed everything. I told them about how I was getting up in the middle of night driving and not even knowing about it. But I thought I was testifying to the glory of God.

"Lord, I thank you because I could've killed somebody," I stood at the front of church and cried. "I could've gotten killed not knowing I was driving Lord! They told me I cut myself one hundred and thirty six times and was pronounced dead on arrival, I thank you Lord!"

I know some people may say, *how can you say thank you Lord for cutting yourself 136 times?* I can say thank you Lord because if I was that out of it I could've sliced my face open, "That's why I thank you Lord!" My children were in the house and if I was that out of it, I could've hurt my children. "That's why I say thank you Lord! It could've been worse!"

People looked at me and saw all of the cuts all over my body but it could've been worse. Even if Sean did it, he could've did worse damage. He could've totally disfigured my whole face. But all I have now is my face and it could've been worse.

After my testimony the church people took it and ran with it. They made the situation so much worse. A Sister got up the very next service and testified, "Well I don't have a story like Sister Bianca, you know, how she lost her mind and all." *What do you mean how I lost my mind and all? I didn't lose my mind!* They were running around the church saying, "Oh Bianca is crazy. Bianca is mentally insane. She's a fruit cake."

I already couldn't get any help from licensed professionals but damn, I couldn't even get any fucking help in the house of the Lord! They made it worse when all I was trying to say was "Lord, I thank you." All you could do as my Brothers and Sister was go behind my back and say "She's crazy?" You couldn't see the blessing?

When I got home from church I fell on the floor and cried to my children.

"I should've never gave that testimony. Do you hear how they are talking about me?"

"Don't worry about it Mama," they patted me on my back.

So when I say help was not available to me nowhere, I mean help was not available to me no... where. Somehow I had to find help within myself. I had to want it bad enough to come off the drugs. To see my kids, they were the ones' who made me want to get straight enough to know what the hell was going on around me. I wanted to get straight because I didn't want them to grow up like I did. I never want to see my kids hurt from child molestation! That's why I sent my kids to Florida right after that. Thirty days later I left my home and moved back to Florida myself.

Chapter 15

God Forbid, I'm Back Home

I knew moving back to Florida wasn't going to be easy, especially since I had to move back in with my mother and Elder Cooley. Right before I had gotten married he kicked me and the kids out of his house and now we were living with him again. As bad as being in his house made me feel, I had to take it because I didn't have anywhere else to go. I'm pretty sure Elder Cooley felt the same way but he didn't say anything about it. Actually, he didn't say too much of anything to me while I was there and that was just fine with me.

But I did do a lot of talking with my mother while I was living there. I asked her why she let us grow up around so much domestic violence and she had the nerve to tell me it didn't happen. Like I was crazy and imagining everything. Then I asked her did she know about Elder Thomas molesting me as a child and she told me "No!" She acted shocked and as if she didn't believe me and that only pissed me off. It was like she just assumed I went around lying about shit like that.

Sometime later I even revealed this to my Aunt Donna. I was telling her in a way like, *you don't have to believe me! If my own mother doesn't believe me then why should you?* I was talking that way because my family is real close to Elder Thomas and his family. Then she told me, "Bianca, I believe you because he did it to me when I was a little girl." What kind of shit is that? And he's still doing it right now!

Elder Thomas has a granddaughter who's the same age as I. We used to play growing up and right now she's a full blown dyke. She has a bald fade like a dude and everything. I remember her mother *(Elder Thomas' daughter)* used to come to church faithfully then all of a sudden she stopped coming and I never knew why.

One time when I was little and was still being molested by Elder Thomas, I went over to her house for diner in-between Sunday services. After dinner she took me on her back patio porch.

"Bianca, has Daddy ever touched you?" she asked me.

"No Ma'am," I lied to her.

"Are you sure?"

"Yes Ma'am, he never touched me." I was still scared at that time.

"If he does, you make sure you tell me you hear?" I nodded my head not knowing he had molested and raped his own daughters.

Come to find out, she stopped coming to church because she tried to reveal her daddy to her mother because even when she became an adult he still tried to come on to her. And this was his blood daughter. But every since 2000, she started coming back to church. But the man has been raping and molesting his own daughters; raping and molesting his own granddaughters; raping and molesting other kids in the church, boys as well as girls; and the sad thing is, he's still there like he's done nothing.

I used to just sit in church and pray to God, *Lord, this is your house. How do you let people like this exist and continue to scar and wound young people?* It really made me question my faith in God. I thought, *Lord, how could you let this happen? This is your house and a lot of the situations took place right in the bathroom.*

In some of the testimonies of when he molested the little boys, he took them straight into the bathroom and straight up fucked them in their asses. Another friend of mine, we'll call him Roy McDougal, he was one of the victims also. Roy and I were real close growing up and one time I was going into the kitchen area of the church where the restrooms are. And I'll never forget when Roy ran out of the restroom and his eyes were red and teary. I tried to stop him to ask, "What's wrong, what's wrong," but Elder Thomas was coming out of the door right behind him.

When it came to Roy, we were told his father *(Elder McDougal)* told Roy, "You tell us who did this! You tell me and I promise I'll kill him!" Then they said Elder McDougal flipped the script and said, "I don't even want to know because I know I'll kill him." Out of all of the boys Elder Thomas was raping and molesting, Roy is the only one I know whose trying to stay away from that homosexual spirit. He's married now and everything. But some of the other gay boys in the church still calls Roy and tell him, "You know you want it. You know you don't like pussy. You know you don't like fish." Roy just tells them, "Man why don't you stop calling me? You know I ain't like that no more. You know I don't do that no more." But that's a strong spirit to try to fight and I feel sorry for Roy.

Some of the openly gay boys married some girls from Detroit and now one of them is beating the mess out of his wife. In my opinion, that's the only way he can prove his manhood because his manhood was snatched away from his as a little boy. He was done the same way. He was beat on and that's the only way he feels he could be a man: until somebody sit him down and let him know, 'what was done to you was wrong.'

Elder Thomas has another granddaughter name Sandy and everybody knows it's happening to her too. She's just so spaced out. When I came back to Florida we were in the Bishop's Council convention at church and Sandy was sitting right behind me next to her mother, and her mother isn't too far from being spaced out herself. When I saw the expressions Sandy was making I was tapping my aunt on her shoulder and saying, "Look at this little girl! Don't y'all see that something is wrong? How can y'all sit up in church and not see this? Her granddaddy is touching her too!"

Sandy is about twelve years old now but even when she was younger, she was having little incidents where she was caught messing around with other little girls when she would spend the night at their homes. They claimed she'd try to eat their vaginas and even try to have oral sex with the little boys. She was doing a lot of things that kids just wouldn't be doing. And the situation is tripped out because I know it's still happening.

Even with all of this going on, I still went to church every time there was service, hoping that something would change, that my life would change, that somebody would preach about that child molester and have him locked up. But nothing ever happened and I started to feel more and more like crap. Just being there made me feel like I couldn't even trust the people in the "house of the Lord." All of the trust I had in people was gone, and still is. I don't trust nobody. No matter how much I tell a person I kind of trust them I don't. I'm just living right now and that's it. I don't trust nobody in my house and there's nothing they can do that will surprise me. I look forward to people hurting me and letting me down. I don't trust my own mother and as much as I love my kids, I don't trust them either. I look forward to my kids betraying me because I don't trust nobody.

That's why I tried to stay to myself and be by myself. But even with who I am, you think people stayed away from me? Hell no! Even when I told them how I was feeling when I went to church they still pressured me to go. Everybody I've ever known was and is a member of that church so the pressure for me to go was tremendous. I tried on purpose to keep people away from me... and it didn't work. I'd be mean on purpose and it didn't work. I became a totally different person other than who I once was... and I liked who I became... I couldn't even feel... I couldn't have a relationship with a man because there was nothing there for me to give.

I remember when I was at church for the church convention. It was winter time so I was feeling safe because I could wear long sleeves. There was a Sister who knew me and she sat on the side of me and asked, "What happened? The top part of your hand is all cut up. What, you tried to commit suicide or something? Ha, ha, ha!" I just stared at her with an expressionless face and didn't say anything. By the end of the service she said, "You know I was just joking. Were you in a car accident or something?" Still I gave her the same response.

People are cruel and don't care about you. I lived by myself in Detroit and struggled with this all by myself and it was so hard. Now I'm back in Florida and it's even harder. Then on top of me feeling like people were cruel, I was also feeling bad because I didn't have any money to support my kids with or a home that we all could live in. I couldn't even buy them any clothes. Thank God for the Salvation Army because they were who I went to for help with clothing my kids.

I had been calling Sean and asking him to send me some money so I could take care of our kids but he always told me he didn't have anything then he brushed me off. One day I was fed up and called Sean. I told him I was going to call and tell Bishop Duren on him and see what he had to say about it? "Bishop Duren can't tell me shit!" Sean yelled. "Call Bishop Duren, I don't care what he say!"

Sean had never in his life talked that way about Bishop Duren and I couldn't understand why all of a sudden he felt as if Bishop Duren couldn't tell him anything? He'd been telling Sean what to do his entire life and Sean never talked back or questioned it. But later on Sean confided in me and told me he found out Bishop Duren was his father.

I know Sean had to have been crushed when he found out Bishop Duren was his father because it crushed me. All of his life he thought the man who raised him was his father, then come to find out he isn't. That has to be devastating. It tripped me out because now my kids are legally Bishop Duren's grandkids. But what tripped me out the most was the fact that Sean was cheating on me with Bishop Duren's granddaughter, Crystal Duren, who is actually Sean's niece! The man was cheating on me with his own niece and he didn't even know it. But Bishop Duren knew about this and he didn't tell either one of them. That was really messed up. So Sean was basically like forget me and Bishop Duren, and he still continued to avoid helping me financially. So I had to do what I had to do.

I got with a group of Caucasian boys who wanted me to perform at one of their sex parties. I had no idea how wild the parties were, and if I had of known I would've never done it. But because I was so desperate for money, I had to have sex with everybody at the party. They were so violent with me and made me open my mouth as wide as I could while they rammed their penises in the back of my throat. One of them would hold my head tightly and they would take turns ramming it in until I coughed, gagged, then spit up all over the floor.

One by one, guy after guy, for seem like all night. Some of them even choked me so I could gag even more. They got off on making me choke and gag and they were even laughing, yelling and drinking beer the entire time. One guy made me gag so hard that I threw up on the floor. Then they had the nerve to want me to lick the throw up off the floor... what cruel and inhumane treatment. But I had to do what they wanted me to do if I expected to get paid...

I got tied up, choked, slapped, fucked so hard that I thought I was about to die, and all for $250 that I used to take care of my kids with. Doing what I did to make some money made me feel like a worthless piece of shit. And because I was feeling the way I was feeling, I believe it had a tremendous effect on my health. My health was going down fast and there wasn't one day when I wasn't wheezing, weak, depressed and had migraine headaches. I was in and out of the hospital all of the time and each time I had to get a different mental evaluation when they saw the cuts on my body.

I was sent to a psychiatrist who I had to see three times a week. It was about two weeks after my first visit when I finished telling him every detail about my life. When I finished telling him about myself he just sat there and looked at me in amazement. "I have never heard of anything like this before," the psychiatrist told me. "And the most unbelievable part about this is your whole life has been messed up by a **CHURCH!** The place where you were going to for help was the place that was killing you! **AND IT WAS A CHURCH!!!** You should never step another foot back in that place again! Then you should call the police, the Lifetime Movie Network for Women, or the Oprah Winfrey Show and tell your story!"

The psychiatrist and I became really good friends. He diagnosed me as being disabled so I could receive some benefits. "Bianca, you are most definitely disabled," he told me. "I think someone needs to care for you for the rest of your life." After that I applied for Section 8 low-income housing and was approved. I thought it was a blessing that I now had a home I could take my kids to. So despite what my psychiatrist recommended, I kept going to church because I thought things were finally changing. But the more I went to church, the more I saw how things weren't changing and the more depressed I became, especially when I saw Elder Thomas from afar at one of our church meetings.

So I stopped going to church and my reason was "because there are child molesters there." I even told my kids we were never going back to that church again. But still, everybody I knew tried to get me to go back and I told them "No" because there were child molesters there. Everybody I sat down and explained this to were like,

"You mean to tell me the Bishops know about this and Elder Thomas is still there?"

"Yeah they know! And that molester is still there!"

I stayed away from the church for about a year and tried to deal with my issues the best way I could. Every so often I got depressed when I looked at my body in the mirror and saw all of the scars. And the summer time was the worst time because I wanted to wear the same kind of clothes as all of the other females were wearing. But I couldn't show my bare skin in public so I wore pants and long sleeve shirts no matter how hot it was outside. At that point I was just becoming comfortable with walking around my kids in a short sleeve shirt. But as for going out in public like that, I wasn't ready for it.

A year of trying to stay to myself had its ups and downs. When times were down I would always call or go see my psychiatrist. He was my biggest crutch at the time. I even took his personal advice and tried to work on my relationship with my mother because she had been trying to reach me and I had been avoiding her. But my psychiatrist didn't know my mother like I know her because when I finally did talk to her I wished I would've never did it. When I tried to get some answers out of my mother about my life she broke down and told me Elder Thomas was my father.

Do you know how devastating that had to be for me? I was twenty seven years old and had no idea who my father was. Then after twenty seven years she told me some crazy shit like that! I could've killed the both of us! After I had completely taken in what she told me I cursed her out, went into a deep depression, and never spoke to her again. With everything I'd been going through since I moved back to Florida, and plus finding out Elder Thomas was my father; I once again sought out refuge in my medications. I didn't even care about being a junkie anymore and I popped my pills to relieve myself from all of the hurt and pain I was suffering from. I locked me and my kids in my own little world and even shut out my psychiatrist.

About two months had passed. I was feeling really bad about myself and was deeply depressed so I sought out help again. Bishop Ross had just recently died and there was a new head Bishop at the Pentecostal Church of God name Bishop Washington. So I called Bishop Washington and told him I needed to talk to him. He gave me an appointment for that Friday afternoon and I really looked forward to seeing him because maybe he could've possibly helped me. The molestation that happened to me was really fucking with my head and that was one of the things I wanted to talk to him about. And not just the molestation, but the fact that the molester was my father made me want to kill myself. Then on top of that, I had to look in the mirror and see my body... I was just all messed up and needed some kind of help... any kind of help... Lord please, help me...

When Friday came Bishop Washington acted like he was so happy to see me. He hugged me and asked me why haven't I been coming to church? I told him everything, and the main reason why I wasn't going to church was because Elder Thomas was there and when I saw him it brought back memories. When I finished telling Bishop Washington about what happened to me he just sat there for a moment like he couldn't believe what I had just told him.

"Bianca, don't let the devil fool you," was what he told me. "The Lord loves you and I had no idea this had ever went on."

"But Bishop Washington, it happened and Elder Thomas is still here."

"If he ever say anything to you out of the way then you come and tell me."

"Yes Sir."

"The meeting is starting tonight and you need to be here. You were made a Praying Woman in Detroit is that correct?"

"Yes Sir."

"Do you still have your Praying Woman's robe?"

"Yes Sir, I still have it."

"Then go home and put it on. Come back tonight and let the Lord use you."

I went home still depressed but feeling a little better. Bishop Washington had somewhat assured me that everything was going to be alright and my help was at the church. So since I desperately needed some help, I was going back to the same church that caused so many problems in my life, the Pentecostal Church of God.

That evening I put on my Praying Woman's robe like he told me to do. It was an all white robe with a matching white hat. I even told my kids to get dressed for church, even after I had been telling them we were never going back there again because of the child molesters.

Once my robe was on and my kids were dressed, we all caught a ride to church with my mother and Elder Cooley. As I sat in the service in my white robe I started having memories as soon as the service began. I think the robe and the service combined triggered it... being molested in the church bathroom as a child. I thought about it over and over again and even though I didn't see Elder Thomas that evening, it was as if he was sitting right next to me in his sweaty wife-beater T-shirt.

After about forty-five minutes into the service I couldn't sit there anymore. So I walked out and went into the dressing room then took off my robe. I stayed in the dressing room for about thirty minutes feeling a little bit relieved because the robe was off. I even tried to go back and sit in the service but I just ended up leaving right back out and staying outside until the service was over.

When I got home that night I was really depressed. After my kids went to bed I ran my bath water, got in the tub with my eyebrow arching blade in my hand, then I cut myself until my water turned red.

I don't know why I did it... I guess I was just depressed about my life. But while I sat in the tub I didn't feel any pain, not even while I was cutting myself. So therefore I cut my legs, arms, stomach, ribs and my back then I sat there in a tub full of bloody water. When I got out of the tub I called my brother Derrick and told him what I had done. That next morning he and my mother took me to the hospital so I could get some help.

The hospital kept me under a suicide watch for three days, gave me some depression medication then sent me home. I was depressed as hell and high off the medication, so as soon as I got home I popped some more pills then cut myself again. After I finished cutting myself I got on the phone and called some of my friends and told them what I did.

"Bianca, why did you do that?" they shouted in horror.

"I don't know?" I cried when I answered them. "Sometimes I just want to take a razor and slice my face open. It all started when I talked to Bishop Washington because I was depressed. He told me to put on my Praying Woman's robe and come to church. When I did it... I couldn't stop thinking about Elder Thomas..."

Word got back around to family that I cut myself again as soon as I got home. So they sent Derrick over to watch over me. He stayed with me all day and night and never left me alone for one moment. When I went to the bathroom he even stood by the door.

"What are you doing in there?" he yelled from the other side of the door. "It don't take that long to use the bathroom!"

"I'm just using it. I'll be right out!"

The next day Derrick went home to get some clean clothes and he was supposed to come right back. Therefore, as soon as he left my sight and I was alone, I cut myself again...

Epilogue

Bianca lived with her troubled past the best she could. Even though the church stressed her out tremendously she still pressed her way back and once again became an active member of the Pentecostal Church of God... Until one church convention when she stood face to face with Elder Thomas. She was walking into the women's bathroom as Elder Thomas was walking out of the men's bathroom as he held his grandson by the hand.

When their eyes met they both stopped dead in their footsteps and he told her with a sinister grin, "Hey Bianca! I ain't seen you in a long time. You want to come over to my house after church because I ain't been with a young girl in years?" Elder Thomas walked away with his grandson who had the same look in his eyes that she had in her eyes when she came out of the boy's bathroom with him over twenty years ago.

That same night Bianca felt as though she'd had enough. Therefore she took a half bottle of her prescribed medication and washed it down with some gin. Then she ran her bath water and got into the tub with her eyebrow arching blade in hand. Bianca sat there for thirty minutes and thought about what a horrible life she has lived. Then with her left hand, she sliced her right wrist and bled to death in the bathtub.

Bianca was discovered the next morning by her son. He'd just woken up by his alarm clock for school. When he went into the bathroom to get ready for school, he found Bianca sunken down into the tub filled with bloody water...

194

ALSO AVALIABLE FROM PAYROLL PUBLISHING

COMING SOON FROM PAYROLL PUBLISHING

IN STORES 2013